NEW ROUTES IN GEOGRAPHY

Around Britain and Europe

MICHAEL HAIGH

CAMBRIDGE UNIVERSITY PRESS
Cambridge
London   New York   New Rochelle
Melbourne   Sydney

Published by the Press Syndicate of the University of Cambridge
The Pitt Building, Trumpington Street, Cambridge CB2 1RP
32 East 57th Street, New York, NY 10022, USA
10 Stamford Road, Oakleigh, Melbourne 3166, Australia

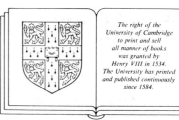

The right of the University of Cambridge to print and sell all manner of books was granted by Henry VIII in 1534. The University has printed and published continuously since 1584.

First published 1985
Reprinted 1987

The map on page 45 may be duplicated for classroom use.

Printed in Hong Kong by Wing King Tong

Library of Congress catalogue card number: 84–17570

British Library cataloguing in publication data
Haigh, Michael
    Around Britain and Europe. – (New routes in geography)
    1. Europe – Description and travel – 1971–
    I. Title II. Series
    914   D967
    ISBN 0 521 28628 X

Acknowledgements

The author and the publisher would like to thank the following for permission to reproduce copyright material:
Dundee University 1, Meteorological Office 30 (table); M Haigh 4, 7, 9, 10 bottom left, top right, 13, 14, 23 bottom, 24 right, 26, 27, 29, 75 bottom left, 86 left; Farmers Weekly 10 top left, middle and bottom right; Saskatchewan Wheat Pool, Regina, Canada 15 top; Royal Netherlands Embassy 15 bottom, 55, 57, 58, 59 left, 60, 62, 63 right, 68 bottom; Danish Agricultural Producers 16, 17, 18, 19 top, middle left, 20 top; Danepak 19 middle right, bottom, 20 bottom; Danish Tourist Board 21 top; IHI Ltd 21 bottom; A Hopkins 22, 65 right, 75 bottom right, 78 bottom, 81, 83, 86 right, 94, 95; West Country Tourist Board 23 top, 24 left; Blackpool Tourism Dept 25 left; British Airways 25 right; Spanish National Tourist Office 28; French Government Tourist Office 30, 31 bottom, 91, 93 left, top right; Townsend Thoresen 31 top; Swiss National Tourist Office 33 top, 34 left, 36, 37, 38 top, 39 bottom, 40, 41 top left, right; Thomas Cook 33 bottom; Bernese Oberland Tourist Office 34 right; Central Electricity Generating Board 38 bottom; Grande Dixence SA 39 top; New Zealand Smelters Ltd 41 bottom left; Shell Photo Service 42, 43, 44, 46, 47, 48, 49, 50, 51; British Steel Corporation 54 top left; ICI plc 54 top right; Redpath Engineering Ltd 54 bottom; Netherlands National Tourist Office 56; Woolwich Equitable Building Society 59 right; Port of Rotterdam Municipal Port Management 61; Sasebo Heavy Industries Co Ltd 63 left; Embassy of the Federal Republic of Germany 64, 65 left, 67 left; German National Tourist Office 66, 68 top; Swedish National Tourist Office 67 right; GEC Computers Ltd 70 left, top right, 73; IBM 70 bottom right, 71, 72; Ford Motor Co Ltd 74 top right, 77 bottom; Vauxhall Motors Ltd 74 left, bottom right, 75 top right; Courtaulds Automotive Products 76 top; Lucas Industries 76 bottom left; Pilkington 76 bottom right; Automotive Products plc 77 top; National Westminster Bank plc 78 top; British Railways Board 80; Overseas Containers Ltd 84; Port of Felixstowe Authority 85; Milton Keynes Development Corporation 87, 88, 89; Vision International 92, back cover; French Embassy 93 bottom right.

Contents

Around Britain and Europe

On 5th April 1981 there was a census to count every person in the United Kingdom. A census form was taken to every home. The census asks many questions and all the answers go into a computer. The census tells us how many people there are and where they live. It also finds out the types of houses people live in, the jobs they do and how they travel to work. This helps to show where new houses, schools, offices, and extra bus services are needed.

The census has been taken every ten years since 1801 (except 1941 during the war). This means we can see changes that have taken place since then. Look at map (1) and the figures in tables (2) and (3). You can see the change in the number of people living in parts of the British Isles and in the ten largest cities.

4 London is Britain's largest city

Many countries in western Europe also had a census in 1981. You can see the number of people in those countries in table (6) on page 6.

1 The British Isles

	British Isles
	United Kingdom
	Great Britain

ATLANTIC OCEAN

SCOTLAND

NORTH SEA

ULSTER

IRISH SEA

EIRE

WALES

ENGLAND

ENGLISH CHANNEL

A B C D E F G H I J

British Isles
United Kingdom
Great Britain

0   100 km

2 Number of people in the British Isles (millions)

British Isles				1931	1981
	United Kingdom	Great Britain	England	37.4	46.2
			Wales	2.6	2.8
			Scotland	4.8	5.2
		Northern Ireland (Ulster)		1.3	1.5
	Irish Republic (Eire)			2.9	3.4

3 Population of the ten largest cities in the United Kingdom (thousands)

	1931	1981
Greater London	8203	6696
Birmingham	1002	920
Glasgow	1088	762
Liverpool	856	510
Sheffield	512	477
Manchester	766	449
Leeds	483	448
Edinburgh	439	419
Bristol	397	388
Belfast	415	374

FOLLOW-UP WORK

1 Look at map (1) and tables (2) and (3).
  (a) How many *more* people were living in the British Isles in 1981 than in 1931?
  (b) In which part of the British Isles did the number of people increase the most?
  (c) With the help of an atlas, name the cities A to J on map (1).
  (d) What change has there been in the size of all the main cities in table (3) since 1931?

2 (a) People went to live in cities because they could get jobs in factories and offices. Now people are moving out of these cities to live in small towns. Wimborne in Dorset, for example, grew from 35 000 to 68 000 people between 1971 and 1981. It is Britain's fastest growing town. Why are people moving from big cities into small towns?
  (b) Ask 36 children including those in your class if they were born in the area or moved into the area where they now live. Draw a pie-graph (divided circle) to show the results of your census. Use the scale
    one person = 10° of the circle.
    What does your graph show?

3 In 1957, West Germany, France, Italy, Belgium, the Netherlands and Luxembourg joined together to form the European Economic Community (EEC). It is often called the Common Market. The United Kingdom, Eire and Denmark joined the EEC in 1973, Greece in 1981, Spain and Portugal in 1986. These twelve countries trade freely with each other but other countries pay taxes (tariffs) when they bring goods to sell in the EEC.
Look at table (6) on page 6 and answer these questions.
  (a) Which country of the EEC has the biggest area?
  (b) How many people were in the European Economic Community in 1981?
  (c) Which EEC country has the most people?
  (d) Which EEC country has (i) the largest, (ii) the smallest amount of its population in towns and cities?

4 With the help of an atlas, match each country on map (7) on page 6 with its largest city from the list below. One in every ten people in Europe lives in these cities. Athens / Brussels / Copenhagen / Dublin / Helsinki / Lisbon / London / Luxembourg / Madrid / Oslo / Paris / Reykjavik / Rome / Rotterdam / Stockholm / Vienna / West Berlin / Zürich.

5 Trace the shapes in diagram (5). Their sizes show the number of people in each country (the larger the shape, the greater the number of people living in the country). Cut out the shapes and fit them together to look like the map of Europe (7).
Look at your 'map' and the actual areas of the countries in map (7). What do you notice about:
  (a) Norway, Sweden and Iceland;
  (b) the Netherlands and Belgium;
  (c) the United Kingdom and West Germany?

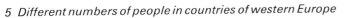

5 *Different numbers of people in countries of western Europe*

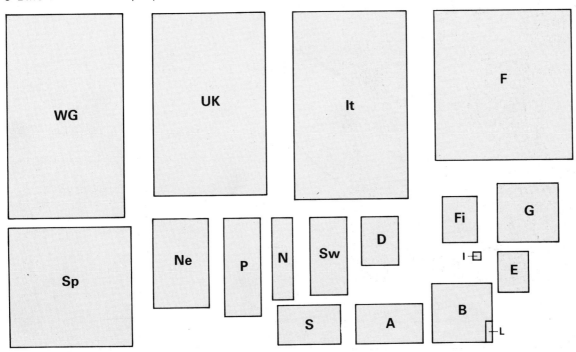

6 Countries of western Europe: statistics (1981)

	Country	Area (thousand square km)	Population (millions)	Living in towns and cities (%)
European Economic Community (EEC)	United Kingdom (UK)	245	55.7	76
	West Germany (WG)	249	61.3	92
	France (F)	547	53.9	78
	The Netherlands (Ne)	41	14.2	88
	Belgium (B)	31	9.9	95
	Luxembourg (L)	2.6	0.4	68
	Eire (E)	70	3.4	58
	Denmark (D)	43	5.1	84
	Italy (It)	301	57.2	69
	Greece (G)	132	9.6	65
	Spain (Sp)	505	37.8	74
	Portugal (P)	92	10.0	37
	Norway (N)	324	4.1	45
	Sweden (Sw)	450	8.3	83
	Switzerland (S)	41	6.3	58
	Austria (A)	84	7.5	54
	Finland (Fi)	337	4.8	62
	Iceland (I)	103	0.2	88

7 Western Europe

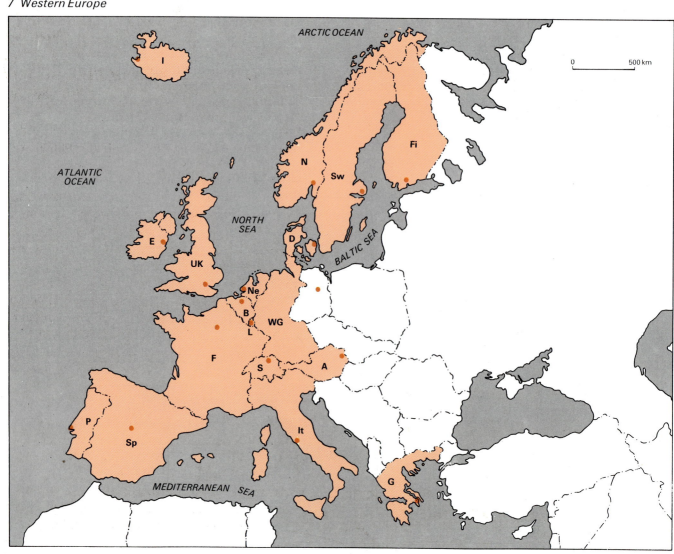

Farming

Changes in the countryside

If you drive into the countryside on a sunny day in summer you will see farmers producing the food we need.

Combine harvesters bring in the grain harvest from large fields. Tractors, fitted with balers, gather up the straw into round bales (1). These are unrolled for the animals to use in winter. Forage harvesters cut the long green grass from the leys. A ley is a field kept under grass for just a few years. The machine chops up the grass and blows it into a trailer (2). This grass is kept green for the animals to eat in winter. It is called silage.

The soil is soon made ready for the next crops. The fields are disc-harrowed, dressed with fertilizer, treated with herbicide and drilled with fresh seed.

You might see a herd of dairy cows in a long line in a field. They are grazing a strip of grass up to an electric fence. You don't see many animals these days because they are kept indoors. Long sheds, with air vents along the roof tops, are for the pigs, poultry and beef cattle. They are fattened up here. Silos, which are very tall buildings, store the food for these animals.

A farmer who has spent all his life farming tells us about the changes he has seen.

'Almost everything has changed since I started farming in the 1920s. I began with eight horses which did most of the work. Three horses in a

2 Forage harvester

1 Bales of straw

plough team would plough an acre in eight hours: today one worker with a tractor can plough an acre in an hour.

'A reaper-binder was used to cut and bind the corn into bundles. These were put on carts and stacked in a big rick until the threshing machine arrived. There were many mice and rats in the rick and we used to have fun chasing and trying to kill them all. They ate a lot of grain and cut the strings on the bundles.

'Three men used to come at 7:00 a.m. to light the fire in the steam engine in the threshing machine. They had steam up by the time another ten men arrived at 8:00 a.m. We worked hard all day until all the rick was thrashed. Today a combine does all these jobs for me.

'In those days most farms were mixed farms with crops and animals. Now most farms are specialised and they grow more crops or keep more animals than ever before. The cost of land, machines and animals is very high and it is now very difficult for a young person to start farming.'

Many changes in farming and the countryside are shown in the sketches on page 8 and table (3) on page 9.

1930

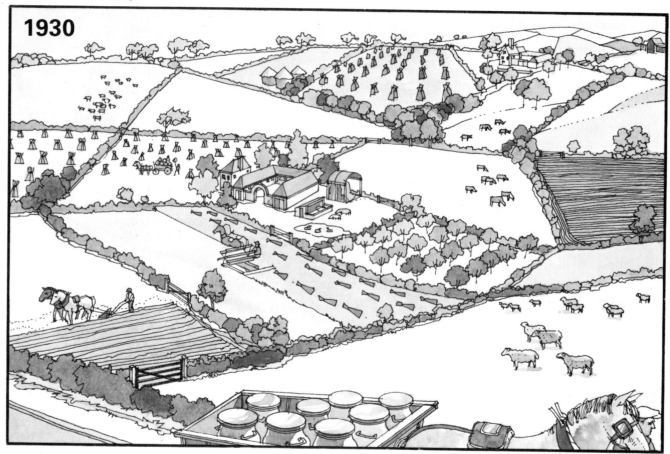

1980

	1930	1980
Cultivated land	13 million hectares	12 million hectares
% under crops	45%	55%
% under grass	55%	45%
Number of farms	500 000	250 000
Number of workers	1 000 000	500 000
Average size of farm	25 hectares	100 hectares
Farm power	750 000 horses	500 000 tractors
Land for wheat	500 000 hectares	1 500 000 hectares
Wheat yield per hectare	2 tonnes	6 tonnes
Chemical fertilizers used	little	2 million tonnes
Cattle	8 million	13 million
Sheep	24 million	31 million
Pigs	3 million	8 million
Poultry	62 million	135 million

Crops or caravans?

FARMING QUIZ

Many farming terms are used in this topic. Test your knowledge 'on the farm'. Ask your teacher for details.

FOLLOW–UP WORK

Look at the two sketches on page 8. The top sketch shows a scene in the countryside in 1930. The bottom sketch is the same area fifty years later.

1 Make a list of all the differences which you can see in the two sketches.
2 How can you tell that:
  (a) farms were bigger in 1980 than in 1930;
  (b) some cultivated land has been lost;
  (c) fewer workers are needed on the land;
  (d) this is a mixed farming area;
  (e) crop rotation takes place;
  (f) methods of raising dairy cattle, pigs and poultry have changed;
  (g) the farmer sells more milk now than in the past?
3 Why are dairy cattle kept closer to the farm buildings than the sheep?
4 Say why it might be a good or bad thing when farmers take away hedges.
5 Which country scenery, 1930 or 1980, do you like best? Say why.
6 The artist who drew the sketches was facing north.
  (a) Why is a farm on a south-facing slope good for farming?
  (b) How can you tell that the wind blows from the west?

Look at table (3) and answer these questions.
7 How can a million hectares of cultivated land have been lost between 1930 and 1980?
8 How many tonnes of wheat were grown in 1930 and 1980? Give two reasons how more wheat is now grown.
9 Explain how more animals are now kept, but with less grassland.
10 Farmers now use a lot of machines. How has this affected:
  (a) the size of farms;
  (b) the use of horses;
  (c) the number of farm workers?

You can see many changes in farming in a journey across England from west to east. Find the five farms on map (9), page 11, and read about them on page 10.

Farming across Britain

Farm A is 80 hectares of sloping land facing south over Mount's Bay near Penzance in Cornwall. The soils are shallow and stony on granite rock. Many local farmers keep dairy cows but this farmer likes to grow crops. The land is used for early potatoes (4), cauliflowers, cabbage, strawberries and daffodils. These are sold all over Britain. There are four workers on the farm.

4 Early potatoes in Cornwall

Farm B is on sloping land near Totnes in Devon (5). This land is also rocky and the soils are thin and full of stones. Most of the 100 hectares are for grass and the farmer has 60 dairy cows and 120 sheep. The cows graze the fields near to the milking parlour and the sheep use the other fields. Lambing is in January and February and fat lambs are ready for the market in June and July. Twelve hectares are used for forage crops such as oats, barley, mangolds and cabbage. There are four workers on the farm.

5 Devon grassland

Farm C is on the hills near Dorchester in Dorset (6). The land is chalk rock and this quickly soaks up the rainfall. Grass is grown on the slopes for 70 beef cattle and 200 sheep. The animals are kept in the same fields. The cattle eat the long grass and the sheep crop the grass close to the ground. The ewes have lambs in March and fat lambs are sold in July and August. The flat fields on the top of the hills, 200 metres above the sea, need a lot of fertilizer to grow barley. This is fed to 60 pigs which are kept indoors. Twenty-four of the 117 hectares on this farm are for crops. There are two workers.

6 Dorset downs

Farm D is 240 hectares of land on the chalk hills near Orpington in Kent. It is 150 metres above sea-level. The soils need a lot of fertilizer for crop growing. This is a 'pick your own' farm (7). These are the fruit and vegetables you can pick:

June/July: strawberries, gooseberries, raspberries, blackcurrants.
June/Aug.: garden peas, broad beans, french beans.
July/Sept.: courgettes, marrows, potatoes, runner beans.
Aug./Oct.: plums, apples, pears, sweetcorn, cabbage.
Sept./Oct.: blackberries, cauliflowers.

There are five workers on the farm.

7 Pick your own strawberries in Kent

Farm E is 600 hectares of gently sloping land in Norfolk (8). There are some sandy soils and some clay soils. The land is used for crops. The main crops are wheat, barley, sugar beet, peas, beans and oilseed rape. There are 1400 pigs and 30 000 poultry. These are kept in special buildings. There are 26 workers on this farm.

8 Harvesting in Norfolk

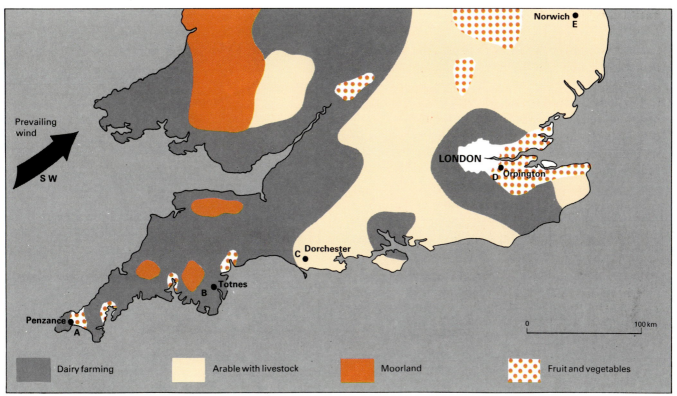

9 Five farms in England

10 Weather statistics for the farms

| | Average rainfall in a year | Rainfall in spring (Mar/Apr) | Rainfall in late summer (July/Aug) | Average temperatures (°C) | | | | | | | | | | | |
				Jan	Feb	Mar	Apr	May	June	July	Aug	Sept	Oct	Nov	Dec
Farm A	1098 mm	146 mm	154 mm	7	7	8	10	12	15	16	16	15	13	10	8
Farm B	898 mm	122 mm	127 mm	6	6	7	10	12	15	17	17	15	12	9	7
Farm C	926 mm	125 mm	133 mm	3	3	6	8	11	14	16	16	14	11	7	4
Farm D	642 mm	84 mm	118 mm	3	4	6	8	11	14	16	16	14	11	7	4
Farm E	630 mm	82 mm	125 mm	3	3	6	8	11	15	17	17	15	11	7	4

FOLLOW–UP WORK

Look at map (9) and the weather statistics (10) to do these questions.

1 Farms B and C are pastoral farms and farms D and E are arable farms. Why are the farms in the west best for grass and farms in the east best for crops?

2 Farms C and D are at about the same height on chalk downs but farm C is pastoral and farm D is arable. Why?

3 Farms A and D grow fruit and vegetables.
(a) Why can farm A sell crops earlier in the year than farm D?
(b) What is the main reason farm D grows crops?
(c) Why does farm A grow crops when many farms nearby keep dairy cattle?

(d) Why does farm D grow more types of crops than farm A?

4 Farms B and C rear sheep.
(a) Why does farm C need more rain to grow good grass than farm B? (Hint: rock.)
(b) Why can lambs be born earlier on farm B than on farm C?
(c) Why are the sheep kept in the same fields as the cattle on farm C but in different fields on farm B?

5 (a) What do you notice about the size of farms as you go east?
(b) Why do you need a big farm to grow cereal crops?
(c) Farm C is bigger than farm B but has fewer workers. Why?

11

Arable farm in East Anglia

Farm E on map (9) is Abbot's farm near Norwich. It is a big farm. 520 hectares are for crops and 80 hectares lie under buildings and trees.

The land is undulating which means it has low rounded hills and shallow valleys. There are heavy clay soils on the upper slopes and light sandy soils on the lower slopes. The clay was laid on top of the sand when an ice sheet covered this land 200 000 years ago. Since then rivers and streams have cut through the clay into the sand below (11).

Wheat, beans and rape are grown in the clay soils and barley, sugar beet and peas in sandy soils. The farmer has a crop rotation for each soil.

Clay soil			Sandy soil	
Year			Year	
1	Rape		1	Sugar beet
2	Wheat		2	Barley
3	Wheat		3	Barley
4	Beans		4	Sugar beet
5	Wheat		5	Peas
6	Wheat		6	Barley
			7	Barley

Crop rotation helps to keep the soil fertile. Different types of fertilizers are used for each type of soil. The farmer uses his own 15-tonne lorry to bring fertilizers from Ipswich or King's Lynn (12).

Peas are grown for Birds Eye Foods factory in Lowestoft. Birds Eye send the seeds to the farmer and tell him when to plant, spray, use fertilizer and harvest. Twenty-six farms in East Anglia work together as one harvesting group. They share machinery and plan to keep a steady flow of fresh peas going to the factory (15). Look where the farmer sells all the things from his farm in table (13) and map (12).

The farm has a lot of workers and machines as you can see from tables (16) and (17). Look at the jobs on the farm, month by month, in table (18).

11 Soils and crops of Abbot's farm

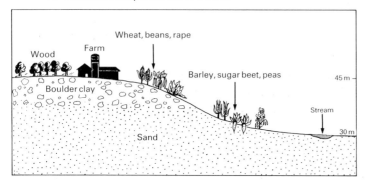

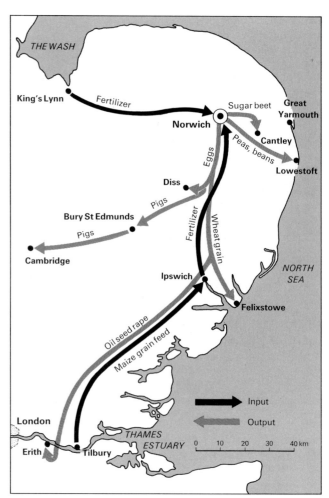

12 Supply and distribution routes

13 Farm products

Product	Uses	Market
Wheat	Flour for bread and biscuits	Flour mills in Norwich and Felixstowe
	Seed	Farmers in East Anglia buy it
	Animal feed	Fed to his own pigs and poultry
Barley	Seed	Farmers in East Anglia buy it
	Animal feed	Fed to his own pigs and poultry
	Beer making	Norwich brewery
Sugar beet	Sugar	British Sugar Corporation factory at Cantley on the river Yare
Peas	Quick frozen food	Birds Eye Foods factory at Lowestoft
Beans	Cattle feed	Sent to Europe via Lowestoft
Rape	Cooking oil, margarine and cattle feed	Crushers at Erith on Thamesside
Pigs	Pork, bacon, ham, sausages and pies	Farm Kitchen Foods near Bury St Edmunds. Some to Cambridge
Poultry	Eggs hatched for chickens	Golden Produce Hatcheries at Diss

14 Flour mill in Norwich

16 Farm workers

	Number
Tractor drivers. They do all the work on the land	8
Poultry keepers	6
Egg cleaners, packers and graders	4
Pig keepers	3
Grain worker	1
Mechanic and fitter	2
Lorry driver	1
Office staff	1

17 Farm machinery

	Number
Tractors	20
Trailers	4
Large ploughs	2
Disc harrows	3
Power cultivators	2
Corn drills	2
Sugar beet drill	1
Set of rolls	1
Muck spreaders	2
Fertilizer spreader	1
Sprayers	2
Combine harvesters	2
Sugar beet harvester	1
Baler	1
Bale handler	1
Fork lift trucks	2

Barn Machinery: Corn dresser, dryer, elevator, conveyer, mills, fan coolers, automatic feeders, grain mixers, cuber to compress meal for pigs.

15 Birds Eye factory, Lowestoft

18 Calendar of farm jobs

January February	Ploughing. Trim hedges. Clear ditches. Tree planting. Overhaul machinery. Winter holidays.
March April	Drill spring barley and sugar beet. Early weed spray programme. Main topdress of fertilizer for winter wheat and barley.
May June	Complete weed spray programme. Fungicide spray programme. Hoe sugar beet. Tidy verges. Trim tree plantings.
July August	Harvest grain crops and peas. Sell seed corn. Buy and apply sugar beet fertilizer. Fumigate grain store.
September October	Clear up straw after grain harvest. Ploughing. Drill winter wheat and barley. Trim hedges. Begin sugar beet harvest.
November December	Sugar beet harvest. Ploughing. Muck spreading. Trim hedges.

Pig and poultry jobs are not tied to any time of the year. Pigs are reared and sold throughout the year. Three times a year the poultry buildings are cleaned out, scrubbed and disinfected and new chicks replace old flocks.

FOLLOW–UP WORK

Study Abbot's farm and then answer the ten questions on page 14. For each question write down the answer you think is best from (a), (b), (c) and (d).

Your teacher will tell you the marks you have gained. Add up your marks and see how you would rate as a farmer.

Points	How you rate as a farmer
25–30	You will make an excellent farmer.
20–24	With training and practice you will do well.
15–19	Average. You will need to work hard.
Under 15	Poor. But keep trying if you are interested.

1 Hedges have been taken down and some big fields have two types of soil in them. Should you:
   (a) use the best soil for crops and the other soil for grass;
   (b) grow one crop in the whole field;
   (c) grow two different crops in the same field;
   (d) only use the best soil in the field?

2 For crop rotation the farmer needs different crops and a six-or-seven-year plan. Should you:
   (a) keep to the present crop rotation plans (page 12);
   (b) only grow the crop which brings most profit;
   (c) grow one crop on the clay soil and one crop on the sandy soil;
   (d) change to cattle and put all the land under grass?

3 It is the fifth year in the rotation on clay soil. Wheat has just been harvested. Should you:
   (a) chop up the wheat straw and plough it back into the soil;
   (b) burn the straw, loosen the soil with a disc-harrow and plant another crop of wheat right away;
   (c) make the straw into bales and plough the soil deeply, letting the winter frost break it up;
   (d) get the field ready for sugar beet?

4 An excellent crop of sugar beet has been harvested from a field near the stream. Should you:
   (a) autumn drill a crop of barley in this field;
   (b) spring drill a crop of barley or peas;
   (c) grow another crop of sugar beet;
   (d) spring drill a crop of wheat or beans?

5 Chemical fertilizers are used to get more and better crops. Should you:
   (a) use crop rotation and animal manure but save money by buying little fertilizer;
   (b) spread a lot of fertilizer to store up nutrients in the soil;
   (c) spread a fertilizer made up of nitrates, superphosphates and potash with the same amount for each field;
   (d) test the soil in each field and use a fertilizer to suit the crop to be grown there?

6 It is late August. Many fields of grain are ready to harvest but the weather is wet. Should you:
   (a) give the farm workers a day or two off work;
   (b) harvest the crops;
   (c) give the workers indoor work until the weather improves;
   (d) spread fertilizer in the sugar beet fields?

7 You belong to a group of farmers supplying peas to Birds Eye Foods. Should you:
   (a) join with other farmers to harvest and market *all* your farm products;
   (b) join with other farmers to harvest and market *some* other crops, perhaps sugar beet and rape;
   (c) do *all* your own harvesting and marketing;
   (d) continue as you do at present?

8 You have twenty tractors, ten of which are old. Should you:
   (a) sell your old tractors and keep the ten modern ones;
   (b) keep all the tractors, but fit one piece of equipment to each tractor;
   (c) hire tractors when you need them;
   (d) start a tractor museum and invite children to visit from schools?

9 Some poultry have a disease. Should you:
   (a) kill the diseased birds;
   (b) clear out the whole flock and get new chicks;
   (c) leave the diseased birds because your usual restock takes place in a few weeks;
   (d) clear out all the flock and just keep pigs?

10 There are 40 hectares of deciduous woodland on the farm. Should you:
   (a) leave the woodland in its natural state;
   (b) remove the woodland and grow more crops;
   (c) cut down old trees and plant fast-growing pines for timber;
   (d) look after the woodland by taking out old trees, growing new ones from seed and planting some more on other parts of the farm?

19 Abbot's Farm on a wet day in August

Food for Britain

Britain's farmers supply about half the food we eat, and we import the rest. Crops like coffee and bananas grow in a hot climate and we have to buy these from other countries. Even though 80 per cent of our land is farmed, this does not produce all the food we need. For example, we have to buy extra wheat from Canada (20), beef from Eire and lamb from New Zealand. We also agree to buy food from other countries we could grow ourselves. We could get all the sugar we need from sugar beet grown on our own farms but we have agreed to buy cane sugar from countries such as Mauritius and Fiji. Since Britain joined the Common Market in 1973 we have bought more food from Europe (21). Look at table (22) which shows Britain's shopping list for food.

20 Wheat growing area of Canada at harvest time

FOOD FOR BRITAIN GAME

This is a game which shows where we buy our food and how it reaches Britain. The game is played by two players using a game board, a dice and shaker, and six coloured counters per player.

Each player has to bring six cargoes of food to Britain. The products are shown in the baskets and the producing countries are on the map.

21 Vegetable growing area of the Netherlands

22 Where Britain shops for food (year ending August 1982)

Food shopping list	British farms (% of what we need)	World market (% of what we buy from other countries)	Cost (£ million)
Bacon and ham	50%	Denmark (67%), Netherlands (20%), Eire (9%)	420
Butter	40%	New Zealand (40%), Denmark (25%), Eire (17%), Netherlands (11%)	360
Beef	80%	Eire (54%), Botswana (10%), Australia (7%), Netherlands (7%)	300
Sugar	40%	Mauritius (38%), Fiji (15%), Jamaica (10%), Swaziland (8%)	270
Lamb	60%	New Zealand (98%)	240
Cheese	70%	Eire (30%), Netherlands (16%), Denmark (16%), France (10%)	240
Wheat	70%	Canada (86%), USA (5%)	210
Tea	—	India (26%), Kenya (25%), Sri Lanka (11%), Malawi (10%), China (5%)	210
Apples	40%	France (45%), South Africa (24%)	150
Coffee	—	Ivory Coast (17%), Kenya (16%), Brazil (15%), Uganda (14%)	150
Cocoa	—	Ghana (40%), Nigeria (31%), Ivory Coast (14%)	120
Potatoes	90%	Netherlands (37%), Cyprus (23%), Egypt (16%)	90
Bananas	—	St Lucia (17%), Colombia (13%), St Vincent (10%)	90
Tomatoes	40%	Netherlands (46%), Canary Islands (33%), Spain (10%)	90
Oranges	—	Israel (30%), South Africa (26%), Spain (15%), Cyprus (11%)	60

Food from: E.E.C. countries 46%   Total in one year 3000
Other countries 54%

Denmark

1 Bacon bound for Britain

Food for Europe

Denmark sends a lot of bacon, ham, butter and cheese to Britain (page 15). Photograph (1) shows a container of bacon ready to be sent to Britain from the port of Esbjerg. Although Denmark is a small country, most of the land is good for farming. Because only 5 million people live in Denmark, there is plenty of food to sell to other countries.

When Britain and Germany became industrial countries in the nineteenth and early twentieth centuries they could not grow enough food to feed all the people working in factories in the cities. Wheat was brought from America, and Denmark sent meat, butter and cheese. Denmark joined the Common Market with Britain in 1973 because it wanted to keep selling food to Britain. Map (2) shows who buys Danish food.

Map (3) shows Denmark is a peninsula and islands. About 18 000 years ago a sheet of ice over

300 metres thick covered what is now Denmark. Look back to page 12 and see how this also happened to eastern England. Masses of boulders and clay at the edge of the ice now forms the hills down the middle of the Jutland peninsula. When the ice melted it left the land covered in clay. As the melt-water flowed into the sea the level of the sea rose and drowned the lowlands. The higher land is now the islands of Denmark. Water streaming

2 Food exports from Denmark

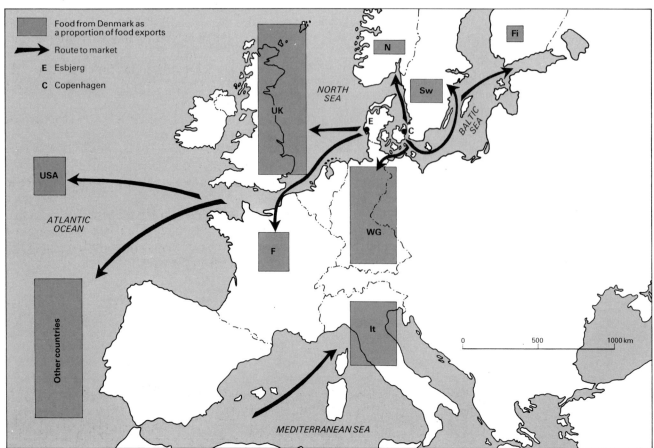

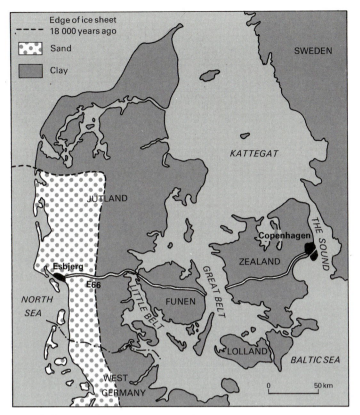

3 Denmark

4 Danish Red dairy cattle

down the Jutland hills washed all the fine sand onto the west side of Jutland. Farms on the sandy soils in the west are different from farms on the clay land in the east. Remember the different uses for the sand and clay soils on the farm in eastern England.

The sandy soils in the west of Denmark are poor but farmers make them better with fertilizers. This part of Denmark is wet. West winds coming over the North Sea bring 800 mm of rain a year. The land is used for growing grass and fodder crops to feed dairy cows. Farms are small with about 10 to 50 hectares and 20 to 50 cows. The cows are in the fields in summer and indoors for the six months of winter when the grass stops growing (4). Milk is collected every day by lorries from the local dairy. Most milk is made into butter.

The clay soils on the east of Jutland and on the islands are better. It is drier to the east of the hills

and summers are hotter than in the west. Barley is grown to feed pigs. Farms are about 30 hectares and have about 100 pigs. One or two pigs go each week by lorry to the local bacon factory.

FOLLOW-UP WORK

1 Use map (2) to answer these questions.
   (a) Which three countries buy most food from Denmark?
   (b) Why can Denmark easily get food to Britain and West Germany?
   (c) Why does most food come to Britain from the port of Esbjerg?
2 Copy diagram (5). Write words from the list below into the correct box on your drawing. Use map (3) to help you.
   Copenhagen / Esbjerg / Funen / Jutland / Zealand / Great Belt / Little Belt / North Sea / The Sound / Sandy soil / Clay soil.
3 (a) Why is it wetter in the west than in the east of Denmark?
   (b) Why are there more dairy cows in the west and more pigs in the east of Denmark?
   (c) Why do dairy cows spend half the year indoors?
   (d) Why are pigs kept indoors all the time?
   (e) Which farms in Denmark are most like Abbot's farm in eastern England, those in the east or those in the west?

5 Section across Denmark

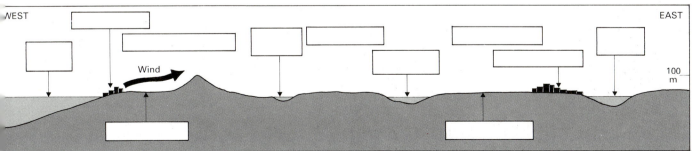

Co-operatives

Most farms in Denmark are small (6) and run by a family. For more than 100 years, farmers have grouped together to process and sell their farm products. The first co-operative dairy was opened in 1882 and the first co-operative bacon factory in 1887. Now there are 200 dairies (7) and 36 bacon factories. These are owned by the farmers.

Farmers send all their milk and pigs to their co-operatives. In return they get a share of the profits from the sale of butter and bacon.

6 Farming landscape

7 Co-operative dairy

There are also co-operatives to supply farmers with feed and seed, fertilizers and equipment. All the farmer has to do is to telephone the co-operative and a lorry is sent with the things that are needed.

Sketch (8) shows that the small farmer is at the centre of a network of co-operatives which together get food from Danish farms to supermarkets in Britain. The story of bacon from farm to supermarket is shown in the photographs on page 19.

8 A network of co-operatives

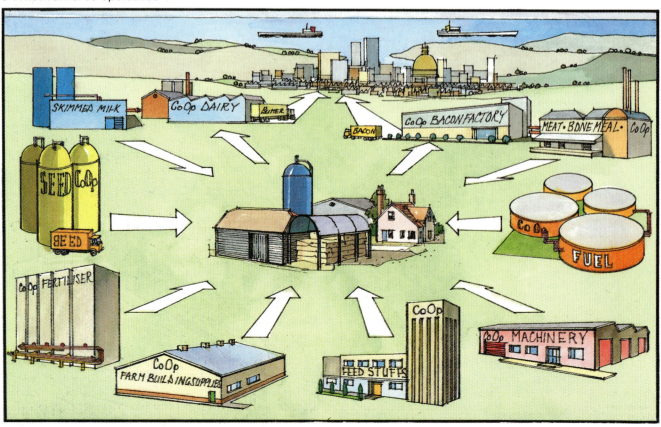

1 The Danish Landrace pig has a long back, small bones and lean meat. The litter is kept in a gentle heat. The pigs grow quickly on a diet of barley grain and skimmed milk.

2 When the pig is six months old and weighs 90 kg, it is taken to the bacon factory. The pig is killed, cleaned, cut down the middle, and injected and soaked in brine for four days to become bacon.

3 Bacon sides are packed in refrigerated containers and taken to the port of Esbjerg. Each week 4000 tonnes of bacon comes to Britain, 60 per cent to Grimsby, 25 per cent to Harwich and 15 per cent to North Shields.

4 The bacon is sliced and packed in Britain. The Danepak factory in Thetford has 1100 people and prepares 600 tonnes of bacon each week. The bacon comes through the port of Harwich.

5 At the Thetford bacon factory 40 per cent of the bacon is smoked. It is hung on racks and smoked in a kiln. Another factory at Selby prepares bacon which comes through Grimsby.

6 Machines slice the bacon at a rate of 650 rashers a minute. The rashers are vacuum packed ready for the supermarket. Thetford supplies southern England, and Selby supplies northern England.

Farming, trade and industry

Denmark is a farming country, but it also has modern factories. It used to export just food but now manufactured goods make most profit (9).

9 Exports

Exports	% of total by value	
	1938	1981
Agricultural goods	80	25
Manufactured goods	18	70
Fish and fish products	2	5

Denmark has no coal, iron ore or other metals. Farming gives the raw materials for industry. You have already seen how bacon is made in factories. Photograph (10) shows butter being made at a dairy. The machinery for making butter is made in Denmark. Photograph (11) shows the machines which pack rashers of bacon. There are more factories which make fertilizers and farm machines.

The Danes have been sea-faring people for more than a thousand years. They make ships for their own trade and for other countries (14). There are eight big shipyards (15), and other factories make engines, radar and equipment to fit into the ships.

Most factories are small and there are some in every part of Denmark including Copenhagen which is the capital, biggest city and port (12).

In recent years oil (1972) and gas (1984) has been found in Denmark's area of the North Sea. This gives power and materials for more industry.

10 Making butter

11 Packing bacon

FOLLOW-UP WORK

1. Copy the sketch of the co-operative network on page 18. Colour the input arrows green and the output arrows red.
2. (a) Why do Danish farmers need co-operatives?
   (b) Why are there more dairies than bacon factories?
   (c) How can co-operatives help to keep the prices of fertilizers low?
3. Show the main stages in the story of bacon from farm to supermarket using labelled sketches.
4. Draw column graphs to show Denmark's exports in 1938 and 1981. Use the figures in table (9). What do the graphs show?
5. Look at this list of things made in Denmark.
   Bacon
   Beer
   Brewery machinery
   Butter
   Butter-making machinery
   Canning machinery
   Cement
   Cheese
   Chocolate
   Farm buildings
   Farm machinery
   Fertilizers
   Freeze-drying equipment
   Furniture
   Ham
   Herbicides

Household electrical goods
Ice-cream making equipment
Insulin
Leather
Marine engines
Motor vehicles
Ship computer equipment
Paper
Pesticides
Pottery
Radar equipment
Refrigeration units
Sausages
Ships
Textiles

Make a table like (13) and put each product in its correct column.

12 Copenhagen

13 Table for question 5

Products made for the farm	Products made from farm output	Machinery to process food	Shipping industries	Others

6 Write about the main types of industry in Denmark. Use your table to help you.
7 Why is it a good thing to have factories, like the shipyards (15), in many parts of the country?
8 Why will North Sea oil and gas help Denmark's industry?

14 Making ships in Denmark

15 Where ships are made

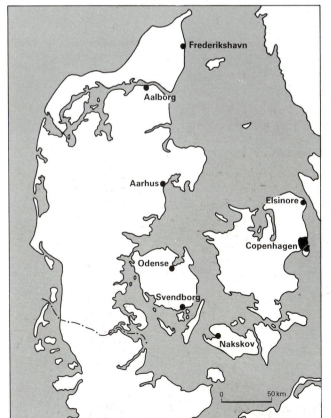

The countryside for leisure

You have seen how Britain and Denmark use most of the land for farming. More and more land is also needed for buildings and roads. Altogether there is very little wild countryside left. People want some open moorland and lovely coastline where they can enjoy the scenery. People need places to walk, climb, ride horses and see animals and birds. Map (1) shows where this is still possible in Britain, in the National Parks. Each park has a committee which has the job of taking care of the area and helping people to enjoy it.

National Parks are not owned by the nation. The land belongs to somebody but you can go across the open moor or along paths and bridleways.

Photographs (2) and (3) show some of the scenery in the Lake District and Snowdonia National Parks.

HOW THE PARKS ARE THREATENED

Many things threaten National Parks. Ask your teacher for details.

1 National Parks

NORTHUMBERLAND
Newcastle
NORTH YORK MOORS
LAKE DISTRICT
YORKSHIRE DALES
Leeds
Manchester
Sheffield
PEAK DISTRICT
SNOWDONIA
Birmingham
PEMBROKESHIRE COAST
BRECON BEACONS
London
Cardiff
Bristol
EXMOOR
DARTMOOR

Parks
Cities
0   50   100 km

2 Snowdonia

3 Lake District

22

Dartmoor: using a National Park

Dartmoor is a wild moorland in south Devon (4). The pinnacles of granite rock that are dotted all over the moor are called tors. These are big blocks of rock that the weather can only slowly wear away (5). Dartmoor is bleak and wet and you can quickly get lost in the mist and fog. The soils are thin and there is only poor grass, heather, gorse and bracken.

Prehistoric remains tell us that people lived here more than four thousand years ago. They kept sheep and cattle just like the hill farmers today. There are 40 000 sheep, 7000 cattle and 2000 ponies roaming the moor.

Most of Dartmoor is owned by the Duchy of Cornwall. The rest belongs to farmers and landowners such as Devon County Council, the Forestry Commission, the Water Authority and the Ministry of Defence.

Dartmoor became a National Park in 1951. A committee deals with plans for new developments. It also looks after visitors to the moor.

DEVELOPMENTS ON DARTMOOR

Imagine that you are a member of the National Park committee. You have to decide *for* or *against* each of these plans for developments on Dartmoor. Write about each plan and give reasons why you were for or against it.

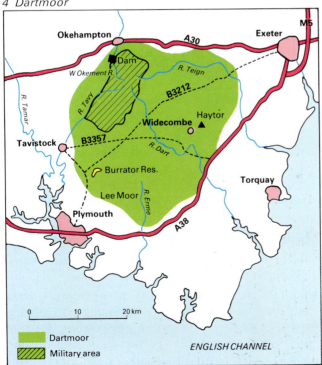

4 Dartmoor

5 Dartmoor tor: Haytor

Tourist facilities

Eight million people visit Dartmoor every year. Most people who spend a summer holiday in Devon visit Haytor and the village of Widecombe-in-the-Moor, made famous by a Devon folk-song.

Plan Permission is needed to build more car parks, toilets, cafés, souvenir shops, picnic areas and refreshment caravans for tourists. These developments will bring jobs to some of the 30 000 people who live on Dartmoor.

6 Widecombe

China clay mining

China clay is decomposed granite rock. The clay at Lee Moor in southern Dartmoor is the best in the world. The clay is used to make paper and pottery. Most of the clay is exported.

China clay is mined at the surface using high-powered jets of water. Waste sand forms the tips (7). Mining has been allowed on five square kilometres of Lee Moor since 1958.

Plan The china clay company wants more land for mining. The company will plant trees around the mine and make the pits and tips into a tourist recreation area when the mine closes.

Military roads

The army has used Dartmoor for military training since 1873. Sixty-four square kilometres of the northern moor (4) are used for firing live ammunition. The area has military roads, barracks and look-out huts.

7 China clay pit and tip

8 Making moorland into farmland at Widecombe

Plan The army wants to make wide roads at the south and east of the training area. These roads will be for army vehicles which until now have caused many traffic jams near Okehampton.

The new roads can be used by cars and coaches to reach the middle of Dartmoor which you can only reach by walking at the moment.

Water supply

There is heavy rainfall on Dartmoor and the rivers give water to the towns and cities of Devon (4). Burrator reservoir was made as early as 1898 to supply water to Plymouth. There is now a shortage of water. This is mainly in summer when there are a lot of visitors.

Plan The Water Authority wants to build a concrete dam across the West Okement river near Okehampton. The valley is narrow here and it will be cheaper to build on Dartmoor than at a site downstream. The reservoir will supply north Devon with all the water it needs.

Farm improvement

Hill farmers are making a poor living and some have sold their farms and left Dartmoor.

Plan A group of farmers want to improve their land by ploughing, liming, fertilizing and sowing fresh grass seed. Two hundred hectares of moorland near Haytor (8) will be fenced off and used for rearing sheep and cattle.

24

Holiday resorts

Although more and more people go to the National Parks for recreation, most people go to the seaside for their main holiday. In the seventeenth century some small fishing villages became the first holiday resorts. They were called watering places where people could drink sea-water to clear their bowels before having a bath in sea-water or a dip in the sea. The idea came from doctors as a cure for ill health, like drinking and bathing in the mineral spring waters at popular spa towns like Bath and Tunbridge Wells.

Scarborough was one of the first fishing villages to become a seaside health resort. A mineral spring was found there in 1626. Only places which could be reached along the roads or by river became resorts. Scarborough was easy to reach from the Yorkshire woollen towns and Brighton easy to get to from London (1). Only rich people with time and money for leisure went to the seaside. Working class families needed all their money to buy food.

In the second half of the nineteenth century railways were built to all parts of Britain. Steam engines which powered machines in the factories were also used to pull carriages full of people to the seaside. Industrial cities were dirty, overcrowded places with poor houses and poor sanitation where people often became sick. Seaside resorts had fresh sea air and gave people a chance of better health.

The idea that working people needed a holiday came with the Bank Holiday Act in 1871. This gave a new holiday in August. Many people in the north of England went to Blackpool (2). Here there were

1 Most visited holiday resorts in Britain

plenty of entertainments, the Tower and illuminations. Blackpool was a place to enjoy yourself, not just improve your health.

Motor cars came onto the roads in the first half of this century. People started to travel far and wide to find pleasant and perhaps less-crowded parts of Britain to spend a holiday. The most popular resorts today are shown on map (1).

After the second world war jet planes brought Spain and other countries of Europe within easy reach. Now people travel to all parts of the world for a holiday. Compare this with people at the start of the century who would have found a fifty-mile journey a great adventure.

2 Blackpool

Jet travel to all parts of the world

A holiday resort in Cornwall

3 Bedruthan Steps, Cornwall

The north coast of Cornwall has some of the best scenery in Europe (3). Because it is in the west of England this coast has never been easy to reach from cities such as London. A railway bridge was built across the river Tamar in 1859 and the main line opened to Penzance. This linked Cornwall to the rest of England. Branch lines were built between 1876 and 1899 to five points on the north coast. These railways caused the growth of five holiday resorts.

The sketch (5) shows part of the north coast of Cornwall. The burial mounds and ramparts (A) were built by tribes who lived there three thousand years ago. Silver and lead were mined on the hill between the sixteenth and nineteenth centuries. The engine house and miners' cottages (B) are still there. The harbour was built in 1850 to export china clay and shelter fishing boats. Pilchards were once caught in large numbers. The Huer's house (C) was

4 The huer's house

used as a look-out point to spot shoals of fish in the bay (4). Fish were stored in barrels in the fish cellar (D). There is only shell fishing now. These days china clay is exported from south coast ports but the old railway line still carries passengers. Fishermen and farmers live in the cottages (E) (6) and there is an old inn (F) by the river.

Imagine your family lives in the house on the cliff top (G) and owns most of the land you can see. You have to decide how to develop a holiday resort.

It is the year 1900. The first development is a large hotel. Choose *one* of the sites marked 1 to 20 to build the hotel. Say why you chose this site.

It is 1920. The hotel is packed with visitors. The old roads have been improved and there is a new bridge across the river. Choose one site for each of these.
1 One area of villas (big houses) for wealthy people.
2 A housing area for local people.
3 An area with shops, bank and offices.
4 An area with three large hotels.
5 Golf links.
6 A theatre with gardens around it.

It is 1950. The villas have been made into hotels and more developments are needed. Choose one site for each of these.
1 An area of guest houses.
2 Another housing area.
3 An area of gift shops, cafés and cinema.
4 An area with gardens, boating lake and children's playground.
Give reasons for your decisions.

5 Develop a resort

It is the present. None of the earlier developments can be changed except the golf links. The town needs modern developments.

1 Choose two sites for new housing estates.
2 Select five developments from the list below which you would like in your town. Choose one site for each development.
  Holiday camp.
  Camping and caravan site.

6 Fishermen's cottages

Two blocks of flats.
Sports centre with swimming pool.
Leisure centre with amusements.
Zoological gardens.
Fairground and circus.
Multi-storey car park and supermarket.
Museum and gardens.
Country park with nature trails.
Clubland and discos.
Conference centre with a big hall in it.
Write about the things you choose.

FOLLOW-UP WORK

1 Draw a sketch to show what your resort looks like now.
2 Choose a name for your town. Design a poster to attract people to it.
3 In what direction did your resort grow? Say why.
4 What sites did you *not* use? Why?
5 Why is it helpful to have all the shops and entertainments close together?
6 Why do many of these places close in winter?

A holiday in Spain

Perhaps you are one of the millions of people who have gone abroad for a holiday. Most people go to Europe (7). Spain is the most popular country to visit and Benidorm the most popular resort. Forty million people visited Spain in 1981, four million of these from Britain. Everybody looks forward to the hot sunny weather, the sandy beaches and the warm sea.

Benidorm was just a small fishing village in the 1950s. Since then it has become Spain's most popular holiday resort. In 1962 there were 20 000 visitors, 200 000 came in 1972 and 2 million in 1982. Benidorm is on the Costa Blanca which means 'White Coast' (14, page 30). The beaches have white sand, some of which has been brought by ship from the Sahara desert. Find this in your atlas. The weather in summer is like the desert with scorching heat and clear blue skies. Hills shelter the town from any winds coming off the land (8).

Benidorm is easily reached by plane. The airport is at Alicante which is a one-hour coach drive from the town. Travel companies provide package tours which give the air flight and a stay in a hotel or flat

7 Holidays abroad from Britain

Country visited	%
Spain	25
France	13
Greece	7
Italy	7
USA	6
W. Germany	5
Ireland	4
Malta	4
Rest of the world	29

for a low price.

The scenery of the coast and hills, the sea, the heat and sunshine are natural attractions. Benidorm also has many artificial attractions. The hotels have swimming pools and evening entertainment. The town has English pubs and clubs, a bull-ring, roast chicken, beefburger and chip counters, gift shops and discos. Benidorm means 'sleep well' but you may not be able to do this because music lasts long into the night. Older people from Britain usually visit Benidorm during the autumn, winter and spring seasons, when the resort is quieter and cheaper.

8 Benidorm, Spain

Bournemouth: a health and pleasure resort

Bournemouth, like Benidorm, is a holiday town and more than a million visitors go there each year. But the two resorts are very different. Benidorm is a jumble of concrete hotels and blocks of flats (8). Bournemouth was planned as a health resort for invalids and a pleasure resort for wealthy people. It is now a popular resort for families (9).

9 Bournemouth sea front

The first building in Bournemouth was an inn built in 1809 for travellers on the road across the heath between Poole and Christchurch. In the 1810s a few cottages were built near the mouth of the river Bourne and let out to visitors. This was the start of a new town.

The land was owned by two or three people who planned Bournemouth as a health resort. Pine trees were planted in the sandy soils and gardens laid out along the river (10). A hospital and large villas were built. The resort was small and peaceful. Then came the railway. The first line reached Bournemouth in 1870 which brought Londoners to the town in only 2½ hours. The town grew quickly after that as you can see in table (11). Hotels and guest houses, parks and gardens, theatres and cinemas, restaurants and cafés, shops and leisure centres have all been added to the resort.

10 Gardens along the river

11 Growth of Bournemouth

Year	Population
1851	700
1871	6 000
1881	17 000
1901	60 000
1931	117 000
1981	145 000

FOLLOW-UP WORK

1 Look at map (1) on page 25.
   (a) Which is the nearest holiday resort to:
       (i) Birmingham; (ii) Manchester;
       (iii) Newcastle?
   (b) Why do you think Newquay became a popular holiday resort later than the other resorts on the map?
   (c) Why has the use of the motor car helped more places to become resorts than the railway did in the last century?

2 Read pages 28 and 29. What would you like and dislike about going for a holiday to:
   (a) Bournemouth; (b) Benidorm?

3 Look at map (14) on page 30.
   (a) Why can you say Benidorm in Spain is quite near to London?
   (b) Bournemouth and Benidorm are both on south-facing coasts. Why is this a good thing for holiday resorts?

4 Look at table (13) on page 30.
   (a) In which year did most people take a holiday?
   (b) What proportion of all holidaymakers went abroad in:
       (i) 1965; (ii) 1975; (iii) 1981?

5 Look at the weather figures in table (12) on page 30.
   (a) Draw a line graph to show the monthly temperatures for Bournemouth and Benidorm. Use a scale of 1 cm for 5 °C on the vertical axis.
   (b) Draw separate bar graphs to show the monthly rainfall totals for Bournemouth and Benidorm. Use a scale of 1 cm for 20 mm on the vertical axis.
   (c) From a study of your graphs say if the weather in Benidorm or Bournemouth is best for the holidaymaker.
   (d) Which is the best month for weather for a holiday in Bournemouth? Say why.

6 Look at tables (15) and (12).
   (a) Which is the most popular month for holidays in Britain?
   (b) Why is this a poor choice for a holiday in Blackpool?

12 Weather at three resorts

	Blackpool			Bournemouth			Benidorm		
	Av. day temp (°C)	Av. rain a month (mm)	Av. day sun (h)	Av. day temp (°C)	Av. rain a month (mm)	Av. day sun (h)	Av. day temp (°C)	Av. rain a month (mm)	Av. day sun (h)
Jan	4	74	2	4	86	2	11	30	6
Feb	4	54	3	5	53	3	12	20	7
Mar	6	46	4	7	56	4	14	18	7
Apr	8	53	6	9	49	6	16	40	9
May	11	61	7	12	56	7	19	31	10
June	14	58	7	15	48	8	23	12	11
July	16	73	6	17	50	7	25	4	12
Aug	16	96	6	17	65	6	26	14	11
Sept	14	91	4	15	76	5	24	46	8
Oct	11	87	3	12	86	4	19	52	7
Nov	7	86	2	8	94	2	15	36	6
Dec	5	83	1	6	83	2	12	25	6

13 Number of British holidaymakers (millions) 1951–81

Year	Britain	Abroad	Total
1951	25	1	26
1953	25	2	27
1955	25	2	27
1957	27	3	30
1959	28	3	31
1961	30	4	34
1963	31	5	36
1965	30	5	35
1967	30	5	35
1969	31	6	37
1971	34	7	41
1973	40	8	48
1975	40	8	48
1977	36	8	44
1979	39	10	49
1981	37	13	50

14 Routes to the resorts

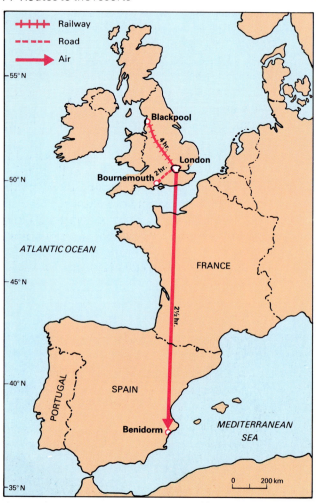

16 Biarritz, France

15 Month of taking main holidays in Britain

May	June	July	Aug	Sept	Others
6%	16%	29%	30%	11%	8%

A trip to France

People who want to tour around Europe in their own car have first to cross the English Channel. Two modern car ferries they can use are seen in photograph (17). Map (21) on page 32 and table (18) can be used to plan a trip to France.

1 Draw a sketch of a car ferry and label any interesting points about it.
2 Which is the shortest crossing of the English Channel to France?
3 A family from Exeter plan a motoring holiday in France. They will spend the first few days in Paris.
   (a) Which is their shortest route to Paris? Name the ports they will use and any towns on the route.
   (b) If the ferry leaves England at 9:00 a.m. when will they reach Paris? Estimate car travel at 60 km per hour on major roads and 100 km per hour on motorways. Add one hour for getting off the ferry, one hour for the difference between time in France and Britain and half an hour for passing through a town.
   (c) Why is Paris a good place to start a motoring holiday in France?
4 A family from London want to drive the quickest route to Cannes (19).
   (a) Name the places along the route they should take.
   (b) It is a long trip so the family needs to stay one night in an hotel. If the ferry leaves England at 9:00 a.m. say where in France they should stop overnight. Explain your choice.
   (c) Say why it will take longer to get to Cannes from Lyon through Grenoble than the other route.
   (d) Why is the shortest route (18) not always the quickest route?

17 Car ferries

18 Shortest routes (in km) from the map

Port of arrival	Destination		
	Paris	Biarritz	Cannes
Santander	1018	281	1113
Roscoff	551	854	1387
Cherbourg	346	810	1245
Le Havre	210	882	1109
Boulogne	241	978	1140
Calais	275	1012	1174

5 A family of four from Birmingham want to reach Biarritz (16) for the lowest cost. They plan for car travel in France at £1 for twenty kilometres without road tolls. They will spend £50 for an overnight stay. The cost of the ferry from each port for the car and passengers on the single crossing is shown in table (20). This chart also shows motorway charges. Which will be the cheapest route? Show your calculations from the ferry port in Britain to Biarritz.

19 Cannes, France

20 Costs of travel

Ferry route	Cost
Plymouth–Santander	£210
Plymouth–Roscoff	£120
Weymouth–Cherbourg	£100
Portsmouth–Le Havre	£100
Dover–Boulogne	£80
Dover–Calais	£80

Motorway tolls	Cost
Calais–Paris	£3
Caen–Paris	£3
Paris–Tours	£5
Tours–Bordeaux	£8
La Rochelle–Bordeaux	£3
Bordeaux–Biarritz	£2
Santander–Biarritz	£4

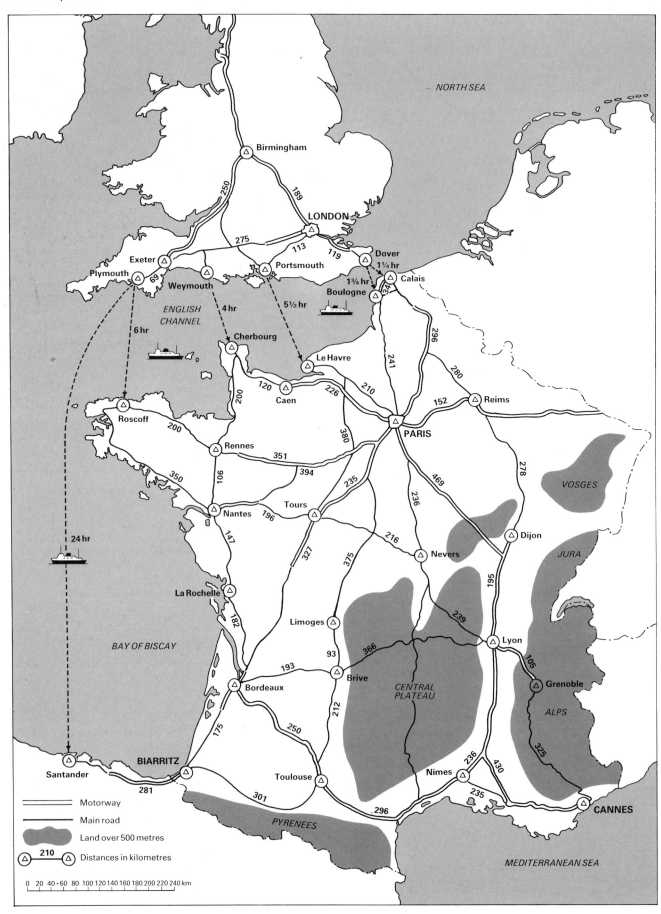

NORTH SEA

Birmingham

250

189

LONDON

275

113   119   Dover
                1¼ hr

Exeter   Portsmouth   1¾ hr   Calais
Plymouth   69   Boulogne
Weymouth   341

ENGLISH   4 hr   5½ hr
CHANNEL   296

6 hr   Cherbourg   Le Havre   241   280

                    120   226   210   Reims
                Caen   152
Roscoff   200   380   PARIS
200
Rennes   278
        351   VOSGES
350   106   469
            394   236
        Tours   Dijon
Nantes   196   235   JURA
                327   375   216
24 hr   Nevers   195
        147
La Rochelle
                            Limoges   239
BAY OF BISCAY   182   93   366   Lyon
                                                    105   Grenoble
                193   Brive   CENTRAL   ALPS
        Bordeaux   PLATEAU
                                212   325
        175   250
                                        236   430
BIARRITZ   Nimes
Santander   281   Toulouse   235
        301   296
            PYRENEES   CANNES

        Motorway
        Main road
        Land over 500 metres
△—210—△ Distances in kilometres

0 20 40·60 80 100 120 140 160 180 200 220 240 km

MEDITERRANEAN SEA

Switzerland

Holidays in the mountains

Six million people visit Switzerland each year. This is a large number when you know Switzerland is one-sixth of the size of Britain and that only six million people live there.

English people made Switzerland into a holiday country. In the eighteenth and nineteenth centuries, English writers and artists saw the beauty of the mountains and lakes and scientists found it an interesting place to study. Until then the mountains, called the Alps, had always seemed unpleasant, dangerous and full of terror for anyone having to cross them.

At the start of the nineteenth century, most visitors to Switzerland went in summer to breathe the fresh clean air of the mountains. Doctors sent their rich patients there to recover from tuberculosis. Small mountain villages with mineral

1 Zermatt and the Matterhorn

2 Tour to Switzerland 1863

springs such as Davos (map (6), square K4, on page 35) and St Moritz (square K5) became popular spas. Other people came to climb the mountains (4).

In 1865 Edward Whymper led a team of British climbers to the top of the Matterhorn (1). The cemetery at Zermatt, at the foot of the mountain, has the bodies of many Englishmen who died in climbing accidents. By the end of the century every peak in the Alps had been climbed.

Many people visited Switzerland on tours organised by Thomas Cook. An advertisement for one of the first tours is shown here (2). Interlaken was the most popular place to visit. This area is shown in picture (3) on page 34 and on the cover of this book.

English visitors started skiing as a winter sport at Mürren at the end of the nineteenth century. Now more than a third of all the visitors go there in winter. Most are from West Germany, France, Britain and America. Map (6) shows there are three areas to visit. The Alps form two ranges of mountains with peaks over 4000 metres above sea-level. The Swiss plateau is a hilly area about 500 metres above sea-level and the Jura mountains, to the north, rise to 1500 metres above sea-level. The map shows five cities. Zürich is the largest and Berne is the capital city.

3 Picture map of area around Interlaken

4 The Alps

5 Lauterbrunnen valley near Interlaken

FOLLOW-UP WORK

1 Use picture map (3) for this question.

(a) Make a list of the interesting things you can see if you stay in this area for a holiday.

(b) The photograph on the cover of this book shows part of the picture map. Name the three mountain peaks in the background of the photograph and the village in the centre.

(c) The Jungfrau railway goes inside the Eiger mountain at Eigergletscher and comes out at Jungfraujoch.

(i) How many vertical metres does the train climb in the tunnel?

(ii) How can a train climb such a steep mountain?

(iii) What other ways of getting high into the mountains are shown on the picture map?

Use map (6) for these questions.

2 (a) Which is the largest region of Switzerland – the Jura, Plateau or Alps?

(b) In which region are all the glaciers? Say why.

3 Lake Brienz is in square F5. Look again at picture map (3).

(a) Name the lake in square E5.

(b) Name the un-named mountain in F5.

(c) In which direction was the artist facing when the picture map was drawn?

4 Rivers flow in all directions from the Alps.

(a) Which river has its source at H5?

(b) Which river flows from the Rhône glacier at G5?

5 (a) Geneva is in square A7. Which squares are Lausanne, Berne, Lucerne and Zürich in?

(b) In which region are all of these towns?

(c) Why do fewer people live in the other two regions?

6 (a) The small inset map shows that Switzerland is a landlocked country. What does this mean?

(b) How can Switzerland have a port (Basle E2) if the country is landlocked?

7 Switzerland has good roads.

(a) Why do the roads follow the rivers?

(b) Why is it easier to build roads from west to east than from north to south?

8 Mountain passes and tunnels help the traffic across the Alps. The 16-kilometre long St Gotthard road tunnel (H5) opened in 1980 and is the longest road tunnel in the world.

(a) To which country does the tunnel give a short, fast route?

(b) Why does the tunnel help trade between Italy and West Germany?

(c) How does this news item for 16th October 1982 help to show why road tunnels are very useful?

Snowfalls block Alpine passes

Berne (Reuter) — Heavy snowfall blocked five Alpine passes in Switzerland — Furka, Grimsel, Klausen, Nufene and Great St Bernhard. Eight others were passable only with snow chains or winter tyres. But access to road tunnels was normal.

Mountain farmers have called in helicopters to rescue sheep and cattle stranded on Alpine pastures.

6 Switzerland

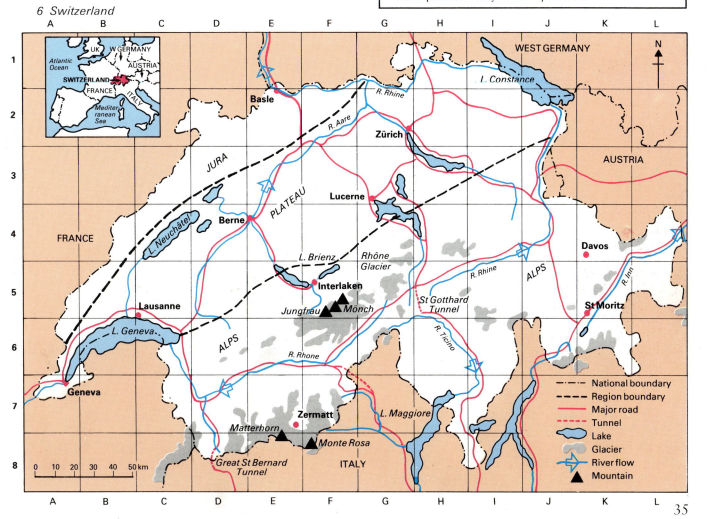

Across a valley in the Alps

You can make a model which shows part of the Alps in Switzerland. Ask your teacher for the two model sheets.

HOW TO MAKE THE MODEL

Piece 1

(a) Cut around the outline of piece 1.
(b) Score along the dashed lines. Bend the sides along the dashed lines to make right-angles. The title will be on the outer side of the base.
(c) Glue the cross-shaded flaps inside the north and south ends.

Piece 2

(a) Cut around the outline of piece 2.
(b) Score along the dashed lines. Bend the side flaps along the dashed lines to make right-angles.
(c) Bend the piece along the dashed lines to make angles which correspond to those on the sides of piece 1.
(d) This piece fits on top of piece 1. Secure into position by glueing the undersides of the flaps on piece 2 to the outer sides of piece 1. Glue the mountain peaks at the ends of piece 2 to the corresponding peaks on piece 1.

Piece 3

(a) Cut around the outline of piece 3. This is a section of the glacier which once filled the valley.
(b) Score along the dashed lines. Bend the two sides on the part marked 'Glacier' along the dashed lines to make right-angles.
(c) Bend the four cross-shaded flaps on these sides inwards to make right-angles.
(d) Bend the long part which is marked with broken rocks underneath to form the base of the glacier.
(e) Secure all the cross-shaded flaps inside the glacier with glue.
(f) Slot the glacier into the glacial trough to complete your model.

Use the model in the work which follows.

How the mountains were formed

The crust of the Earth is split into huge sections called plates. If these plates move against each other there are earthquakes and the rocks fold upwards. One plate can move beneath the other, lifting the folded rocks even higher (7). The Alps were formed like this about 25 million years ago. They are called fold mountains. Write 'Fold mountains' in the box at the south end of your model. Colour the folded rocks. The Earth is 4600 million years old. This means the Alps are young mountains.

7 How the Alps were made

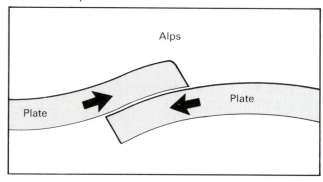

8 A view over the Alps

How a glacier changed the valley

A glacier is a mass of ice which moves down a valley (9). When snow falls on the mountain peaks it does not melt because the temperature is always below freezing. The weight of a fresh fall of snow presses the snow beneath it into ice. The ice moves downhill under the force of gravity and is pushed by fresh snowfalls in the mountains. The ice follows the easiest route, down a valley.

The Aletsch glacier (10) stretches 16 kilometres down a valley in Switzerland. It is the longest glacier in Europe. In the seventeenth, eighteenth and nineteenth centuries the climate was colder than it is now and the glaciers were longer. The model shows how a glacier was once in this valley. The ice sticks to the rocks on the sides and bottom of the valley. Because the glacier moves downhill about twenty metres per day it tears away the rock and carries it along. The boulders help to wear away the valley sides and bottom. Broken rock is shown in the glacier. The rock carried at the side of the glacier is called lateral moraine, that at the bottom is called ground moraine and rock in the middle of the glacier is called medial moraine. Write these three names into the correct boxes on your glacier.

9 Close-up view of the Rhône glacier

Take the glacier off the model. See how the valley is very deep and wide. It is called a glacial trough. It was the glacier which made the valley very deep. Wearing away the rock is called erosion. The river looks very small in this big valley.

FOLLOW-UP WORK

1 Why are old mountains like those in Scotland lower than young mountains like the Alps?
2 Why are rocks like limestone which were formed in the sea now in a range of mountains over 4000 metres above sea-level?
3 How deep is the glacier ice on your model?
4 How can you tell how high the glacier was from the shape of the valley?
5 Valleys formed by rivers are V-shaped in cross-section. How does a glacier change this shape?
6 Why is the valley at X on the south side of the model hanging high above the main valley floor?
7 Many more features caused by ice are shown in photographs (4) on page 34 and (8). The sharp ridge of land which is left between two glaciers is called an arête. A hollow where a glacier begins is called a cirque or corrie. A three- or four-sided peak with glaciers on each side is called a horn.

Draw a sketch of mountain scenery from the photographs. Label as many features as you can.

10 Aletsch glacier

How temperatures change with height

Although the sun is shining brightly and people are sunbathing in the mountains (11), the air around these mountain peaks is very cold. The rays of the sun do not heat the air. It does heat the sunbathers! The ground has to absorb the heat and then it heats the air. But the snow and ice reflect the heat away from these high mountain slopes.

As you climb the mountains the temperature drops at the rate of 6 °C for every 1000 metres. Mark into the boxes on the north side of the model the temperature at 1000 metres, 2000 metres and 4000 metres.

Sunny and shady sides of the valley

In the northern hemisphere the sun is in the south. Imagine the lightbulb in the room is the sun. Point the south side of the model to the light. The valley lies east–west. Notice how the mountains cast a shadow. The slopes that face the sun are sunny and much warmer than the shady slopes. Write the words sunny and shady into the correct boxes on the alp areas of your model.

1 Is the north-facing slope or the south-facing slope the sunny slope?
2 When the model is turned sideways to the light and the valley lies north–south, what do you notice about the sunlight in the valley?
3 Say which side of the valley on your model, sunny or shady, has:
   (a) most farmlands;
   (b) villages;
   (c) most trees;
   (d) the higher treeline (the highest places on the mountains where trees grow).
   Give a reason for each answer.

11 Sunbathing in the mountains

New developments in the mountains

1 *Hydro-electric power (HEP)*
   The power of falling water can be used to make electricity. A dam has to be built to store water in a reservoir (12). Water is led down steel pipes to the power station where jets of water are used to turn turbines. Electricity is generated in dynamos worked by the turbines. A pulp and paper mill is planned on a site near the power station.
   (a) Mark onto your model a site for:
      (i) the dam;
      (ii) the power station and pulp and paper mill.
   (b) Why is this a good place for making:
      (i) hydro-electricity;
      (ii) pulp and paper?
   (c) Why will these developments help the people living in the village?

12 Dam and reservoir in the mountains

13 Dinorwig power station, Wales

14 Upper reservoir at Dinorwig power station

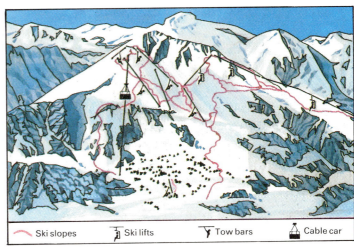

| Ski slopes | Ski lifts | Tow bars | Cable car |

15 Ski slopes at Anzère

(d) What problems will there be for the area?

In 1984 a big HEP station opened in Britain. This is in the mountains of Snowdonia, north Wales. Photographs (13) and (14) show the upper reservoir and the underground power station. Ask your teacher about this power station.

2 Skiing resort

A large holiday company wants to develop the alps on the sunny side of the valley into a ski area. Some of the huts at B on the model will be made into holiday chalets, a ski school, ski shops, bars, coffee shops and restaurants. There will be new blocks of flats, food and gift shops, skating and curling rinks. There will be a cable car from the alp to the village (A). There will be ski lifts and tow-bars on the main ski runs. It will be like Anzère (15).

(a) Mark onto the model where you would put the cable car, ski runs, ski lifts and tow-bars.
(b) Why will the HEP development help this scheme?
(c) Why will this development help the village?
(d) What problems will there be for the area?

Living in the mountains

Most of the people living in the village (A) are farmers. Crops do not grow well because the soils are thin, summers are short and there is heavy rain and snow. Most farmers keep dairy cows. It is very cold in winter and snow covers the ground. The cows are kept inside from November until April. They are fed hay and barley grain.

The best farmland is at the bottom of the valley where the soils are made from moraine left by the glacier and from silt left by the river. Each farmer has a few plots of land dotted about the valley which are used for grass, barley, potatoes and vegetables in summer.

In spring the snow melts and soon the cows are taken by lorry up the winding road to the pastures on the alps (16). The buildings on the model at B are used in summer. Cheese is made here because it is too far to send the fresh milk to the village.

The cows come down from the alps in the autumn before it snows. This movement of animals and people up and down the mountains because of seasonal changes in the weather is called transhumance.

Terraces have been built on the sunny side of the valley. These are built like steps with soil piled behind stone walls. The terraces on your model are vineyards and the grapes are used to make wine.

16 Pasture on the Alps, Grindelwald

39

Imagine that you are a farmer living in the village (A) on the model. Study these details. What would you do? Say why.

1 You are making little money from farming. Should you:
   (a) find a winter job cutting trees in the forests;
   (b) find a full-time job in a factory in a nearby town leaving the rest of your family to do most of the farmwork;
   (c) ask your elder daughter, who is about to leave school, to find work in an office in the nearby town;
   (d) continue with farming as at present?

2 A farming family has gone to live in Zürich. Three plots of land are for sale. These are marked 1, 2 and 3 on the model. You can borrow money to buy one plot. Which would you choose?

3 A farmer friend of yours says he will look after your cattle on the alps in summer. You will have to pay him for doing this job but if he also looks after the animals of another farmer the price will be lower. What will you do?

4 Many farmers who use the alpine pastures want to join together and pay for a plastic pipeline to carry milk from the alps to the village. The fresh milk can be sold in the village and in a nearby town. You will get a monthly payment for your milk. Any milk that is left will be made into cheese at a large dairy in the village. Do you want to join the scheme?

17 Making watches

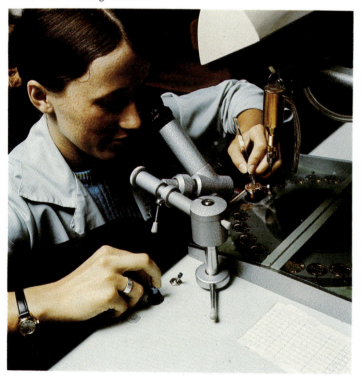

A modern industrial country

When we looked at Denmark (page 20) we saw that most people found work in factories and offices. It is the same in Switzerland. Switzerland is known as a mountain country but most people live in the low areas in towns and cities where they work in factories, offices and shops.

The oldest factories in Switzerland are paper mills which use the trees and water power of the Alps.

Watch making is another old industry. Craftsmen began making clocks in Geneva more than 400 years ago. Farmers who were cut off by snow in the villages of the Jura mountains made watches in the long winters. Longines Watch Company built the first factory in 1867 at Saint-Imier. Switzerland now makes 90 million watches a year and exports most of them. Photograph (17) shows that a skilled person is still very important in this industry. They like to make good watches. They cannot compete with Japan when it comes to making cheap watches.

Swiss cheese, condensed milk, milk powder and milk chocolates all use milk. Most of the milk comes from dairy cows on the plateau. The Swiss eat more chocolates than anyone else in the world. Holidaymakers also take home large amounts of chocolates as presents. Chocolates are made from local milk and cocoa beans from Ghana and the Ivory Coast. You can see chocolates being packed into fancy boxes in photograph (18).

18 Packing chocolates

19 The river port of Basle

Switzerland has no coal or oil or any other useful minerals. All these have to be bought from other countries. Coal comes up the river Rhine from the Ruhr coalfield in West Germany. You will find out more about this on page 66. Coal is used to make drugs, cosmetics, plastics and fertilizers on the riverside at Basle (19).

Aluminium ore (bauxite) comes from Brazil. This goes to factories near the river Rhine and the river Rhône in the Alps. The rivers are used to make electricity which is needed to refine the aluminium. There is a big electrical company at Zürich. It makes turbines and generators for these power stations. Zürich (21) is famous for its banks. Switzerland has a long history of peace and neutrality. Wealthy people from all over the world put their money in Swiss banks knowing it will be safe and secure. Money from banking is used for new industries.

20 Aluminium factory in the Alps

21 Zürich

22 Imports and exports (1982)

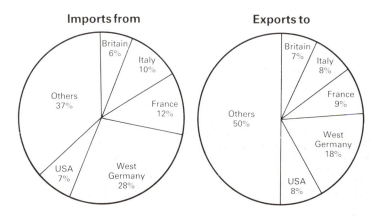

Imports from

- Britain 6%
- Italy 10%
- France 12%
- West Germany 28%
- USA 7%
- Others 37%

Exports to

- Britain 7%
- Italy 8%
- France 9%
- West Germany 18%
- USA 8%
- Others 50%

FOLLOW-UP WORK

1 Why are there:
   (a) chocolate factories on the Swiss plateau;
   (b) watch factories in the Jura mountains;
   (c) aluminium factories in the Alps;
   (d) chemical factories in Basle?

2 What is the link between:
   (a) Ghana and chocolate making;
   (b) West Germany and drug making;
   (c) Brazil and aluminium refining?

3 Look at the trade graphs (22). Why is a location in the *middle* of Europe a good one for an industrial country like Switzerland?

Power for Britain

North Sea oil and gas

We have seen how Switzerland uses its mountains and rivers for hydro-electric power. It was coal that helped to make Britain the most important industrial country in the world in the eighteenth and nineteenth centuries. Now oil, natural gas, nuclear power and hydro-electric power as well as coal give the power for our industries. Britain also earns money from selling oil. The story of how this oil comes from the rocks under the North Sea is an exciting one. This is just a small part of that story.

On 4th August 1975 five tugs pulled the Brent 'B' oil production platform out from the Stavanger fjord in Norway where it was made into the North Sea where it now stands. Photograph (1) shows the 350 000-tonne concrete platform towering 128 metres into the air. Another 80 metres of the legs are below the waves. You can see how big it is when you think that an average-sized house is just 8 metres high.

Brent 'B' is one of four platforms which get oil and gas from the rocks 3000 metres beneath the sea. The field is the area under which the oil is found. View (2) shows the Brent field as you look north from the Brent 'A' platform. Brent 'B' is on the right, Brent 'C' middle left and Brent 'D' in the distance. The photograph was taken through a telephoto lens

1 Towing the Brent 'B' platform

which makes the distance look shorter than it really is. The field is 4 kilometres wide and 16 kilometres long which makes it one of the biggest in the North Sea. The first oil came up in November 1976. These figures show how much oil was won from the Brent field in the first few years.

1976	1977	1978	1979	1980	1981	1982	1983
(million tonnes)							
0.1	1.3	3.8	8.8	6.8	11.1	15.2	18.7

2 The Brent field

Oil wells are holes drilled in rock to get out oil. The drilling is done down the legs of the platform. The drill bit which cuts into the rock is fixed into the end of a ten-metre length of steel pipe. Three lengths of pipe are screwed together and held in the derrick ready to use. The man at the top of the derrick (5) swings the pipes into the drilling position. Thirty metres below on the drill floor the pipes are screwed together to push the drill bit deeper into the rock (6). It takes thirty days to drill a well to 3000 metres. More than twenty wells are drilled from each

3 Drilling for oil

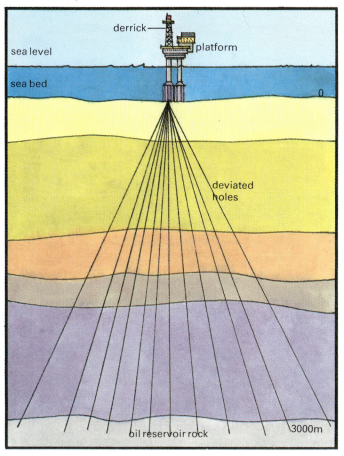

4 Plan view of wells

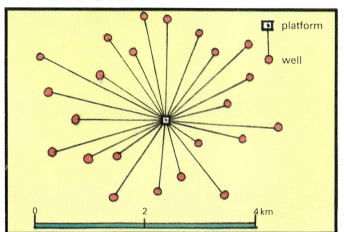

5 View from the top of the derrick

platform to bring up the oil and gas. The holes are drilled at an angle away from the platform to reach all parts of the field. They are called deviated holes (3, 4). Oil comes to the surface under natural pressure and it is very hot (80 °C). Some wells are drilled so that water can be pumped into the rock to take the place of the oil which has come out. This helps to keep up the pressure which brings the oil to the surface.

6 Work on the drill floor

Before all this work could begin the countries around the North Sea had to agree which part of the sea bed belonged to them. Lines were drawn on a map (8) at an equal distance from all the coastlines. They are called median lines. These lines make sectors (areas) for each country. Each sector was split into blocks by latitude and longitude lines at one-degree intervals. Each block was then split into thirty areas. Big oil companies got permission from the government to look for oil and gas in some of these areas. In 1964 twenty-two companies began to explore their areas. The gas and oil they found in the next twenty years was beyond their wildest dreams. British Petroleum (BP) made the first gas strike in October 1965 from block 48/6. This is the West Sole gas field marked with a triangle on map (8). Each area is numbered in the same way. Look at table (7) which gives some details about ten oil and gas fields in the North Sea.

FOLLOW-UP WORK

1 Use map (8) to answer these questions.
  (a) Which two countries have the largest sectors of the North Sea?
  (b) Why do the Orkney Islands and Shetland Islands help Britain get a big share of the North Sea?

2 Put a coloured counter onto the map for each of the oil and gas discoveries shown in table (7). Use green counters for gas and red counters for oil.

3 (a) Where were most gas fields found?
  (b) Where are the oil fields located?

4 Using map (8) and table (7) say why it was easier to get the Hewett field into operation than the Magnus field.

5 Lines of latitude and lines of longitude are used to find places on the map. One gas production platform on the Hewett gas field is 53° 1'N 1° 47'E. Notice there are 60 minutes (') in a degree (°). In which fields are these platforms?
  (a) 53° 4'N, 2° 11'E;   (b) 57° 45'N, 0° 56'E;
  (c) 58° 27'N, 0° 19'E;   (d) 61° 8'N, 1° 42'E.

Brent 'D' towers over the deck of the approaching supply boat

Radio communications dish – a link between the platform and shore

7 Ten oil and gas fields in the North Sea

Date	Discovery (*large)	Location	Water depth (m)	Field name	First production
1966	Gas*	49/26	30	Leman Bank	1967
1966	Gas	48/29	30	Hewett	1967
1966	Gas	49/18	30	Indefatigable	1968
1969	Oil	22/17	90	Montrose	1976
1970	Oil*	21/10	115	Forties	1975
1971	Oil, gas*	211/29	140	Brent	1976
1973	Oil*	15/17	145	Piper	1976
1974	Oil*	3/3	140	Ninian	1978
1974	Oil	14/19	115	Claymore	1977
1974	Oil	211/7	180	Magnus	1983

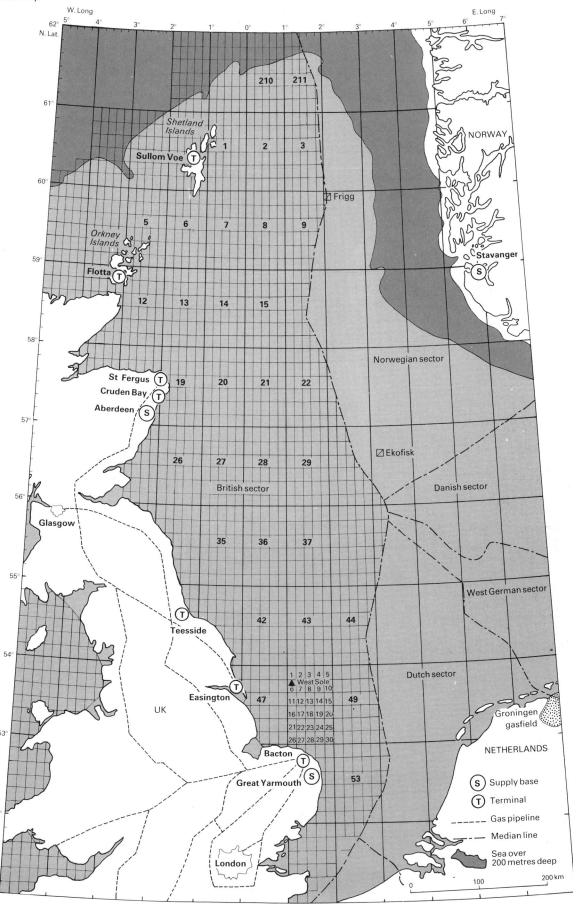

Bringing the oil and gas ashore

Oil from small fields far from shore is put into large ships called tankers which bring it to an oil terminal on the coast. Large oil fields are linked by pipeline to the oil terminal. It costs one million pounds to lay three kilometres of pipeline on the sea bed so the shortest route to the shore is chosen.

Sections of steel pipe coated with tar and sprayed with concrete are welded together on a pipe-laying barge. The pipe is fed out from the stern of the barge (9) down to the sea bed. Pipelines from the Brent and Ninian fields come ashore in the Shetland

10 Laying pipeline on land

9 Laying pipeline at sea

Islands. Photograph (10) shows the pipelines being laid side by side across Shetland. Their route to the terminal at Sullom Voe is shown on photograph (11).

Sullom Voe is the largest oil terminal in Europe. It opened in 1978 and can handle 100 million tonnes of oil a year. Gas and water are taken out of the oil in the process area. The gas is made into a liquid and stored in tanks. Liquefied petroleum gas (LPG) is the 'bottle' gas used by campers. The crude oil is put into big tanks. It is then taken by tankers to refineries around the coast of Britain, to Europe and to other parts of the world.

11 Sullom Voe oil terminal

46

The only way to bring gas ashore is by pipeline. Only large gas fields merit the cost of a pipeline. Small fields are not used. A network of pipelines (8) carries gas around Britain to use in homes and factories.

FOLLOW-UP WORK

1 Use map (8) to answer these questions.
  (a) How far was the Brent 'B' platform towed to the Brent field? Give your answer in kilometres.
  (b) Why has the platform got long legs?
2 Study photograph (12) of the platform. Why does it need to be very strong with the underside of the deck 23 metres above sea-level?
3 (a) Copy the outline of the oil field (13). Mark on four platforms and draw a circle with a radius of 2 km around each one. Draw 20 wells from each platform with a similar pattern to diagram (4). Letter the platforms 'A', 'B', 'C' and 'D' from south to north.
  (b) How many years will it take to drill 20 oil wells and five water injection wells from one platform?
4 (a) The helicopter in photograph (14) is carrying workers from Brent 'B' to Brent 'A'. How far does it travel?
  (b) Why are helicopters the best way to carry passengers between platforms?
  (c) Where on the platform does the helicopter land and take off?
  (d) In what weather conditions would flying be difficult?
  (e) How could a helicopter help in an emergency where someone has been injured and fallen into the sea?

14 Helicopter above Brent field

12 Brent 'B' in rough seas

13 Oil field

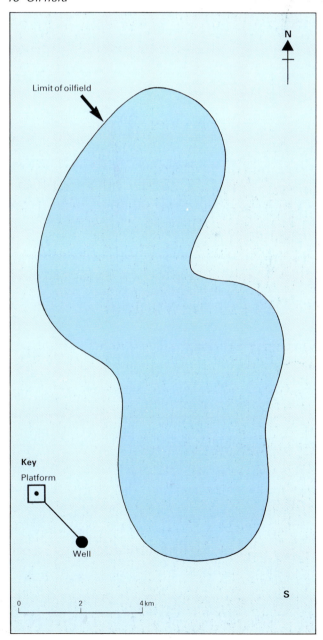

N

Limit of oilfield

Key
Platform

Well

0   2   4 km

S

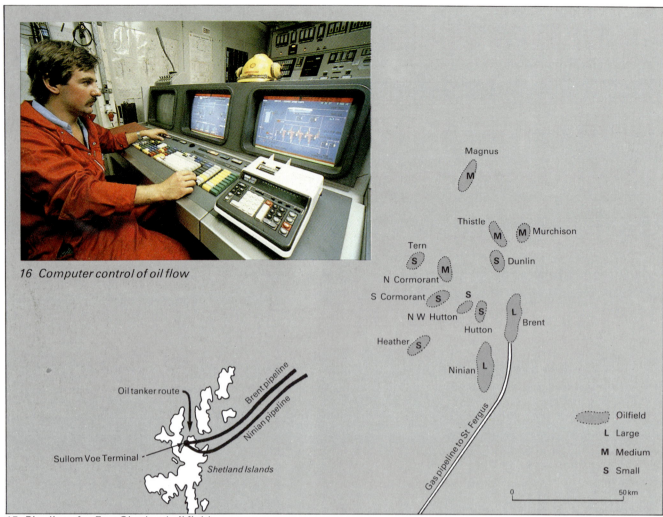

16 Computer control of oil flow

15 Pipelines for East Shetland oil fields

5 (a) Copy the map of the East Shetland oil fields (15). Small and medium-sized fields can be linked by feeder pipelines to the main pipelines from the Brent and Ninian fields. The final sections of the main pipelines are shown on the map. Extend these pipelines to the large oil fields. Link the other fields to them with feeder pipelines. Plan the shortest possible pipeline system to keep the cost down. Many oil companies will share the cost and share the use of the pipeline network you have made.

(b) Photograph (16) shows a computer checking the flow of oil into the pipeline from the platforms on the Brent field. Why is this a good idea?

(c) By looking at map (8) and photograph (11) say why Sullom Voe is a good place for an oil terminal.

(d) Natural gas from the Brent field goes by pipeline to St Fergus. Plot the route of this pipeline on map (8). Why was such a long route to a terminal chosen?

(e) Plot a route from the Frigg gas field to St Fergus.

6 Use map (8) for this question. Match each field in the first column with a terminal from the second column in table (17). Choose short routes.

7 Oil from the Ekofisk field in the Norwegian sector of the North Sea flows along a pipeline to Teesside in Britain.

(a) Plot the route of the pipeline on map (8). How long is the pipeline?

(b) How much would it cost to build?

(c) What stops Norway building a pipeline from Ekofisk to Stavanger?

17 Fields and terminals

Field	Terminal
Brent	Easington
Piper	Sullom Voe
Forties	Bacton
West Sole	Flotta
Leman Bank	Cruden Bay

Building a platform

The giant steel base of a platform is called the jacket. The one shown here (18) makes the buildings of Cherbourg in France where it was built look small. In 1981 the jacket was towed into the North Sea, upended and fixed to the sea bed with steel piles on the North Cormorant field. All this is shown in diagram (19).

There are many steel platforms like this one in the North Sea. The top of the jacket is about 50 metres square. Onto this are stacked about 20 ready-made sections of plant and accommodation called deck modules. The heaviest modules weigh 2000 tonnes. The platform has a drilling derrick, a flare stack for burning unwanted gas, a radio mast, a helideck and cranes.

A MODEL OIL RIG

Your teacher will give you the bits to build your own platform, but only from paper! When you have made the platform answer these questions.

1 (a) What made you decide where to put:
   (i)   the helideck;
   (ii) the medical room;
   (iii) the flare stack;
   (iv) cabin accommodation;
   (v)   power station?
   (b) Why are modules shaped like boxes?
   (c) Why is it a good idea to use modules for building platforms?
   (d) Why does the derrick need to move?
   (e) Why do the modules overhang the base?

19 Taking a 'jacket' to sea

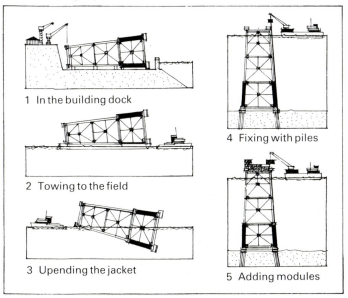

1 In the building dock

2 Towing to the field

3 Upending the jacket

4 Fixing with piles

5 Adding modules

18 Steel 'jacket' towers over houses

2 There are many dangers on a platform. Read this and answer the next questions.

On Friday 22nd April 1977 there was a blow-out on the Bravo platform in the Ekofisk field. A jet of hot oil shot 60 metres into the air drenching the men on the drill floor. A cloud of gas quickly blotted out the sky. One spark would cause an explosion and start a fire which could take months to put out.

The crew of 112 abandoned the platform in minutes. A fire-fighting ship from the Forties field offered help and began to spray water over the platform to reduce the risk of fire. If the oil did catch fire it would soon spread by a chain-reaction to all the wells feeding oil to the platform.

The blow-out happened as workers were fishing down the well for a lost measuring instrument. As oil seeped to the surface a valve, called a blow-out preventer, failed to work because it had been fitted upside down. The release of pressure from below brought the oil and gas to the surface at a speed of 200 miles per hour. 4000 tonnes of oil spilled into the sea every day forming a slick which killed fish and sea birds.

Experts from America worked for days in gale force winds and heavy seas to fit a new blow-out preventer. On 29th April the job was done. By this time 30 000 tonnes of oil and 60 million cubic feet of gas had been lost but luckily nobody had been killed.

(a) Why is a blow-out in the North Sea a bigger problem than a blow-out at an oil well on the land?
(b) What can oil companies and men working on North Sea oil rigs learn from this disaster?

Living on an oil platform

It takes about an hour to reach the Brent field by helicopter from the Shetland Islands. The platform then becomes home for 200 men for the next seven days. Ships from Aberdeen take supplies to the platform. This includes food and drinking water, drill pipes and bags of clay and chemicals for making drilling 'mud'.

The men work twelve-hour shifts from 6 to 6. They have to work very hard, often in bad weather. Apart from those who drill wells there are engineers, electricians, technicians, radio operators, welders, painters, cranemen, cooks and medics. Roustabouts do all the labouring jobs. They all get big wages.

The cabins are not far from the drilling area on this small island in the sea. There is no escape from the noise of machinery, air conditioners and helicopters. Cabins are small with a toilet, shower and washbasin (20). There is plenty of good food which the men can get at any time of the day or night in the dining room. There is a cinema, recreation room, lounge and gymnasium to use in the few hours they are not working or asleep. Men get ill, have tooth-ache and accidents. The sick bay (21) is there to help them.

At the end of seven days the men are ready to spend seven days ashore with their families and friends. This is a welcome change from being stuck in the middle of the North Sea.

20 Two-berth cabin

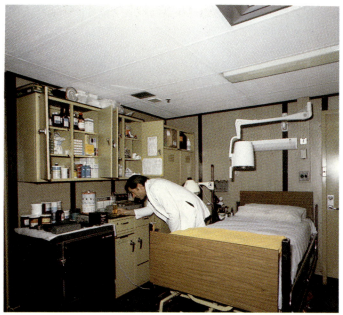

21 Sick-bay

FOLLOW-UP WORK

Write about what you would like and dislike about working on an oil platform.

22 World oil production: top 14 producers in 1983

		Production (million tonnes)	% world
1	USSR	618	22.4
2	USA	487	17.7
3	Saudi Arabia	246	8.9
4	Mexico	149	5.4
5	Iran	124	4.5
6	United Kingdom	111	4.0
7	China	105	3.8
8	Venezuela	98	3.5
9	Canada	77	2.8
10	Indonesia	63	2.3
11	Nigeria	60	2.2
12	Kuwait	54	2.0
13	Libya	52	1.9
14	Iraq	46	1.7

23 Exports of North Sea oil

Country	% of total exports
USA	33
W. Germany	22
Netherlands	15
France	6
Sweden	5
Denmark	5
Others	14

What happens to North Sea oil and gas?

Gas from the North Sea goes into the 5000-kilometre network of pipeline shown on map (8). Half of the gas is used in homes for central heating, cookers and water heaters. The rest goes to factories, power stations, offices and other places.

Britain took 111 million tonnes of oil from the North Sea fields in 1983. This makes Britain one of the biggest oil producers in the world (22). More than half the oil is sold to other countries (23). Britain's refineries (24) take the rest plus some heavy oil from Saudi Arabia and other countries. The refinery breaks down the oil into things we need (25). Oil gives power to factories, heat and light for homes, runs cars and lorries, trains, ships and

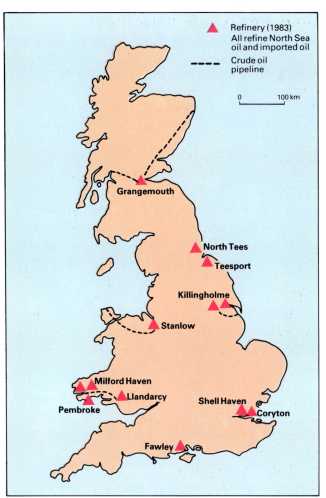

24 Britain's oil refineries (1983)

25 Uses for North Sea oil

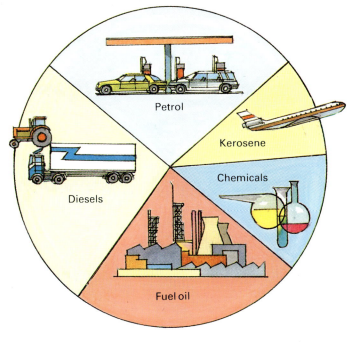

26 Stanlow oil refinery

aircraft. The refinery also makes chemicals for paint and plastics, fertilizers and sprays, rubber and textiles and many other things.

FOLLOW-UP WORK

1 Make a list of ten products in your house which come from oil.
2 North Sea oil gives jobs to a lot of people. What jobs are needed to:
   (a) supply the oil fields;
   (b) get oil from the North Sea;
   (c) use the oil when it comes ashore?
3 Why are oil refineries (24) on the coast?
4 Why does Europe benefit from having oil fields in the North Sea (23)?
5 Britain will get less oil from the North Sea in the 1990s and only a little oil in the twenty-first century.
   (a) Why will amounts get less?
   (b) How should we use the oil we have left?

Class discussion: 'What will we do when the oil runs out?'

Industry on Teesside

Some towns on the east coast of Britain have been helped by the North Sea oil industry. Aberdeen has become a base to supply the oil fields. Industries on Teesside use the oil and help to build oil platforms. Look at map (1) as you read this.

Oil from the Ekofisk field in the North Sea (A on map 1) goes along a pipeline to Teesside (B). Another pipeline carries the oil to the North Tees oil refinery (C). Refined oil products from the refinery go by pipeline to the Imperial Chemical Industries (ICI) chemical works on the south bank of the river at Wilton (D). Textile fibres, polythene, plastics and detergents are made at Wilton. Wilton, the North Tees refinery and ICI's chemical works at Billingham (E) are joined together by two tunnels under the river Tees. Raw materials and products are sent along them.

A pipeline carries oil from the North Tees refinery to the blast furnace at the Redcar iron and steel works (F). Bulk carrier ships bring iron ore (G) to the iron and steel works from Canada, Brazil, Sweden and many other countries which are shown on map (2). Coal (H) from Australia, Poland and the USA is mixed with local coal from the Horden colliery (I) to make a good coking coal for the blast furnace.

Limestone from the Pennines (J) is put into the furnace as a flux to clean the iron. Molten iron is moved in special containers along a railway to the steel works at Lackenby (K). Here steel is made by blowing oxygen into the molten iron to take out carbon and other impurities. Steel is taken by railway to the Redpath Offshore engineering works in Middlesbrough (L) where modules and helidecks for North Sea oil platforms are made. Modules for the Brent 'A' platform were made here. The modules are loaded onto barges and towed out into the North Sea (M).

1 Teesside

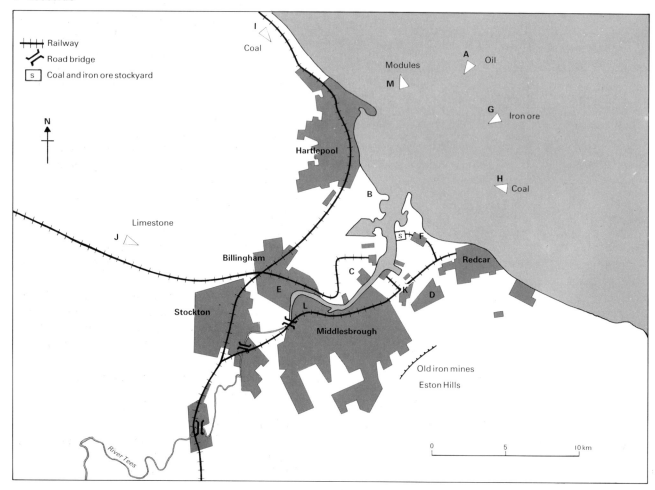

FOLLOW-UP WORK

1 Copy map (1). Draw arrows to show the flow of materials and products between places (lettered from A to M) on the map. Name the raw material or product by the side of each arrow.

The arrows show how one industry depends on another. How does:
(a) the chemical industry depend on the oil industry;
(b) the textile industry depend on the chemical industry;
(c) the oil industry depend on the steel industry;
(d) the steel industry depend on the oil industry?

2 Name three other industries which depend on:
(a) the steel industry;
(b) the chemical industry.

3 *Material input and output for a 10 000 tonnes a day blast furnace*

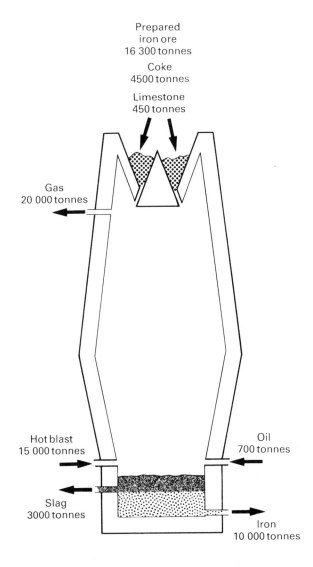

Prepared iron ore
16 300 tonnes

Coke
4500 tonnes

Limestone
450 tonnes

Gas
20 000 tonnes

Hot blast
15 000 tonnes

Oil
700 tonnes

Slag
3000 tonnes

Iron
10 000 tonnes

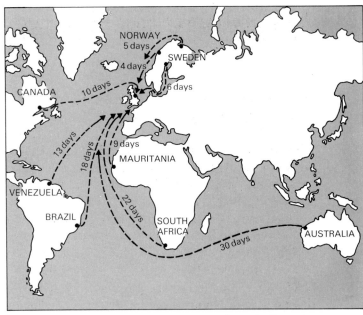

2 Iron ore routes and journey times to Teesside

3 Teesside has had industries for a long time.
(a) The first furnace was built in Middlesbrough in 1851 and there were over 100 along the Tees by the year 1900. Iron ore from the nearby Eston Hills (1) was used in the furnaces between 1851 and 1961. The iron and steel was used for building railways and for engineering. Why is Teesside still a good place to have an iron and steel industry?
(b) The Billingham chemical works was built in the first world war to make ammonia for explosives. The site was near to a coal field, the river and the sea. There was plenty of flat land, skilled people and good road and rail links to other parts of the country. ICI took over the factory in 1919 to make ammonia for fertilizer. Why is Teesside still a good place to have a chemical industry?

4 Iron ore is imported from many countries (2).
(a) Which supplies are:
  (i) nearest to Britain;
  (ii) furthest away from Britain?
(b) Give two reasons why big ships are used to bring iron ore to Britain.

5 Copy diagram (3) which shows how 10 000 tonnes of iron can be made in one day in the Redcar blast furnace. How does the diagram help to show why getting supplies of iron ore is the main task?

6 Say how each of these things help the Teesside steel industry:
(a) a blast furnace near the coast;
(b) the river Tees;
(c) plenty of flat land (some of it has been reclaimed from the sea);
(d) being near to Middlesbrough.

53

4 *Redcar iron and steel works*

5 *Wilton chemical works*

7 A bulk carrier ship unloads Australian iron ore into the stockyards at Redcar (4). Europe's largest blast furnace is top centre and the North Sea top left.
  (a) Where on map (1) was the photograph taken?
  (b) In which direction was the camera pointing?
  (c) Is the bulk carrier on the river Tees or on the North Sea coast?

8 Photograph (5) shows the ICI petrochemical and plastics works at Wilton. The works in the top half of the photograph makes hundreds of thousands of tonnes of ethylene and propylene every year.
  (a) Where on map (1) is this works located?
  (b) Why is plenty of flat land needed?
  (c) What are the buildings near the camera used for?

9 Photograph (6) shows modules for the Beryl 'B' oil production platform in block 9/13 of the North Sea. The module on the right weighs 2200 tonnes and is an 'hotel' for 206 men. The module on the left has a dining room, cinema, galley and recreation area.
  (a) Where on map (1) was the photograph taken?
  (b) About how high is the platform on the right of the photograph?

10 Photograph (7) shows one of the modules being loaded onto a 100-metre barge ready for towing out into the North Sea.
  (a) How is such a large module put onto a barge?
  (b) Which of the two modules is it?
  (c) Is the barge on the river Tees or on the North Sea coast?
  (d) What are the pink beams and steel ropes on top of the module used for?

6 *Two modules for Beryl 'B' platform*

7 *Loading a module onto a barge*

The Netherlands

The Netherlands is a country at the southern end of the North Sea. Gas was found here in 1959. This is the Groningen gas field you can see on map (8) on page 45. Some gas was also found in eastern England. This made people think there might be gas and perhaps oil in the rocks below the sea between England and the Netherlands. This we know was true. Britain found most oil and gas. The Dutch, the name for the people of the Netherlands, have found small oil and gas fields.

The Netherlands and the sea have sometimes been friends and sometimes enemies. The Dutch use sea routes to trade all over the world. There was a golden age of trade in the seventeenth century and there has been a new one since 1950. But the North Sea has struck at the Netherlands many times. Most of the land is low and flat (1). Even the high land is only 80 metres above sea-level (2). In the twelfth century the sea flooded over this low land making the South Sea (Zuyder Zee) (4). Since then the Dutch have been pushing back the sea to get the land that had been lost. The figures in table (5) on page 56 show the land gained each century. Map (3) shows all the land taken back (reclaimed) from the sea. This land is needed because the Netherlands is

1 'Low' Netherlands

2 'High' Netherlands

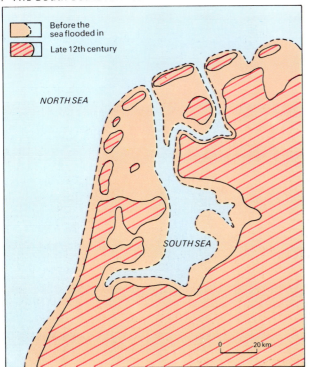

4 The South Sea is formed

Before the sea flooded in

Late 12th century

NORTH SEA

SOUTH SEA

0   20 km

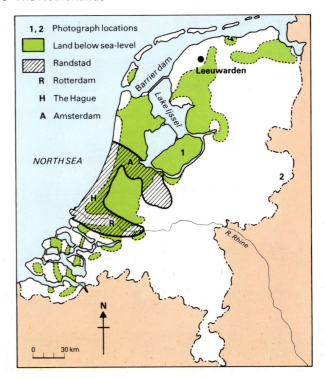

3 The Netherlands

1, 2   Photograph locations

    Land below sea-level

    Randstad

R   Rotterdam

H   The Hague

A   Amsterdam

Barrier dam

Lake IJssel

Leeuwarden

NORTH SEA

R. Rhine

N

0   30 km

one of the most crowded places in the world (6). Look at table (7) which shows the number of people has grown quickly since 1830. This is in a country only a sixth the size of Britain.

A lot of land is taken up by one big city called the Randstad (Ring City). This city includes Rotterdam (a big port), Amsterdam (the capital city) and the Hague, which has the government offices.

The first step to reclaim the South Sea was to build a barrier dam (3 and 8). After a struggle lasting five years the dam was finished in 1932. Now the water had to be pumped into the North Sea. Soon there would be more land to grow food and give the Dutch more space in which to live.

5 *Land reclaimed from the sea*

Century	square km
1200–1300	350
1300–1400	350
1400–1500	425
1500–1600	710
1600–1700	1120
1700–1800	500
1800–1900	1170
1900–2000	2300

8 *The barrier dam*

6 *Average number of people on each square kilometre of land*

Country	Number of people
Netherlands	347
Japan	315
West Germany	248
UK	228
India	208
China	102
USA	24
USSR	12

7 *Population of the Netherlands (millions)*

Year	Number of people
1831	2.6
1931	8.0
1981	14.2

FOLLOW-UP WORK

1 Use map (3) for this question.
   (a) How much of the land of the Netherlands is below sea-level?
   (b) Why is most of this land in the north and west?
   (c) How much of the Randstad is below sea-level?
   (d) Why do you think this city has the shape of a horse-shoe?

2 Use the figures in table (5).
   (a) Draw a column graph to show how much land was reclaimed each century.
   (b) What is your main finding from the graph?

3 Look at photograph (1) which shows land with fertile clay soils and photograph (2) where there are poor sandy soils.
   (a) How can you tell that photograph (1) was taken at point 1 on map (3) and photograph (2) at point 2?
   (b) Write about the differences between the two areas using these headings:
      (i)   the shape of the land;
      (ii) type of farming;
      (iii) size and shape of the fields;
      (iv) where the farm buildings are located;
      (v)   trees;
      (vi) roads.

4 Look at the barrier dam (8) and where it is on map (3).
   (a) What are two uses for the dam?
   (b) The dam has made Leeuwarden closer to Amsterdam by road. Does the new route save 20, 40 or 60 kilometres?

Developing a polder

An area of land reclaimed from the sea is called a polder. It takes a long time to make the sea bed into useful land. The main stages in developing a 50 000 hectare polder are these.

Stage 1 Building a dyke

A dyke is made from clay, sand and stone (9). About 90 kilometres of dyke is needed to circle the 50 000 hectare area. It is called a ring dyke and takes many years to build. It takes less than a year to pump out the sea-water.
Time: seven years

Stage 2 Growing reeds

Reed seeds are sown from a light aircraft into the mud. The reeds help to dry the land, make it firm and keep out weeds.
Time: five years

Stage 3 Drainage ditches and deep ploughing

The reeds are cut or burned when the land is firm. Ditches are cut by machine at ten-metre intervals. Salt water flows out of the land into the ditches. After three years the ditches are replaced by perforated plastic pipes. These pipes carry away rainwater. This keeps the land dry. If there is sand on top of clay, a plough is used to turn up about two metres of clay (10). The mix of sand and clay gives a fertile soil.
Time: three years

10 Deep ploughing

9 Building a dyke

Stage 4 Growing the first crops

The first crops are grown by government workers and not by farmers. Large machines are used to prepare the ground and harvest crops of oilseed rape, flax, peas and grass. Tests are made on the quality of the soil in all parts of the polder.
Time: five years

Stage 5 Laying out farms and settlements

The polder is laid out with farms, woodland, roads, villages and towns.
Time: five years

FOLLOW-UP WORK

1 (a) Draw a sketch showing a dyke being built. Use photograph (9). Write a few sentences about how the dyke is built.
   (b) Why is an aircraft used to sow the reed seeds?
   (c) Why does the government cultivate all the polder for the first five years?
   (d) Draw a column graph to show the time needed for the five stages in developing a polder. Use a vertical scale of 1 cm for two years. What does the graph show?
   (e) With the help of the graph say why polder land is very expensive.

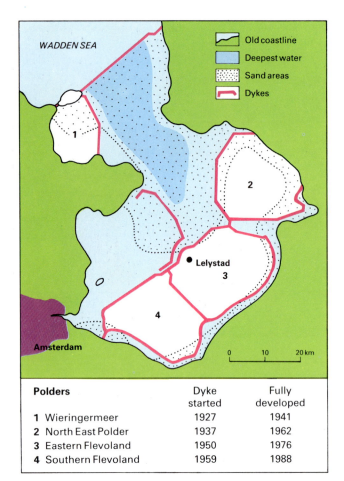

11 Zuyder Zee polders

Polders	Dyke started	Fully developed
1 Wieringermeer	1927	1941
2 North East Polder	1937	1962
3 Eastern Flevoland	1950	1976
4 Southern Flevoland	1959	1988

2 Look at map (11). The Zuyder Zee (South Sea) has gone and there are now four polders and a lake of fresh water (3).
  (a) How much of the Zuyder Zee has been made into dry land?
  (b) Why was the lake made in the north and the polders in the south?
  (c) How can the lake be used? Try to think of three different uses.

3 The first two polders were needed for growing food. The newest polders have more uses. Make a list of all the different uses of the land you can see in photograph (12).

4 Copy map (13) of Southern Flevoland. You have to decide how to use the land.
  (a) Colour two squares in red as housing areas in a new town. The people will come from crowded parts of Amsterdam.
  (b) Colour two squares in brown for industrial estates. These will give jobs to people in the new town.
  (c) Colour six squares in green for recreation. This will include woodland areas, leisure parks, sailing and fishing clubs, picnic sites, camp sites and wildlife areas.

12 Many uses for Eastern Flevoland polder

  (d) Colour all the other squares yellow. This is farmland.
    Treat squares which are less than half-filled with land (e.g. A5) as half squares.

5 Use your map to do these.
  (a) Write a few sentences about the polder you have planned.
  (b) Count the squares on your map. Each square is 25 square kilometres. What is the size of Southern Flevoland? Give your answer in square kilometres.
  (c) How much of the polder is:
    (i) farmland;
    (ii) built-up land (houses and factories);
    (iii) recreation area?

13 Southern Flevoland

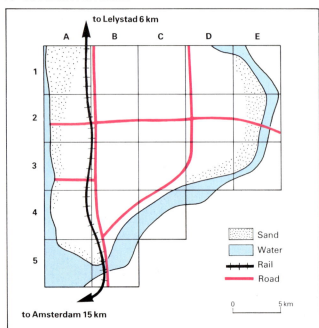

The sea strikes back

During the last night of January 1953 there was a big storm over the North Sea (14). Winds up to 160 km per hour pushed masses of water southwards towards the Netherlands. There was also a high tide caused by a close approach of the moon to the earth. The surges of water crashed against the barrier dam. The dam held and the north of the country was saved from another flood disaster.

It was a different story in the south. Here there is a delta area where three rivers, the Rhine, Meuse and Scheldt, enter the sea. The rivers were running high as the surges of sea-water hit the area. The dykes were broken in 89 places, and 1853 people and 34 000 cattle were killed. Forty-seven thousand houses were destroyed, roads were swept away and 200 000 hectares of land were flooded (15).

As Flevoland was being made in the north, the sea had struck back in the south. Some dykes held and this saved half of the Netherlands from being flooded.

The Dutch decided that a flood disaster like this should never happen again. The barrier dam was made higher and work started on sealing off some of the delta estuaries to keep out the sea.

Britain was also hit by the North Sea storm in 1953. More than 300 people were drowned as low land was flooded. In 1982, a flood barrier for the Thames came into use at Woolwich. A Dutch company with all the skill of keeping out the sea raised the level of the two banks from the barrier dam to the sea. Photograph (16) was taken looking towards the City of London. Look for the concrete piers. Big steel gates come up from the river bed between these piers when a high surge tide is due. The ten steel gates, which were made on Teesside (see page 52), will stop London being flooded ever again. Now look at map (21) on page 84 to see where the barrier dam is.

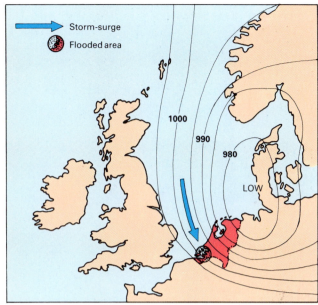

14 Weather map: midnight of the storm

FOLLOW-UP WORK

1 Explain how each of the following things helped to cause the flood disaster:
   (a) the wind;
   (b) the tide;
   (c) the shape of the southern part of the North Sea;
   (d) the position of the Netherlands;
   (e) the rivers;
   (f) the height of the land.
2 Imagine you are a farmer living in the flood area (15). Write an essay about the flood.
3 Which part of Britain was hit by the 1953 storm (14)?
4 Why did London need a barrier on the Thames?

THE DELTA PLAN

You can follow the step by step progress of the Delta Plan. Ask your teacher for details.

15 A scene of the 1953 flood

16 The Thames with its flood barrier

Rotterdam: port for Europe

Most of the Netherlands' trade by sea goes to and from the port of Rotterdam. Rotterdam is the biggest port in the world. The reason is because it is at the centre of one of the world's busiest industrial and business areas. The area a port serves is called its hinterland. The hinterland of Rotterdam is most of Europe. If a circle with a radius of 500 kilometres is drawn around Rotterdam it includes 160 million people, most of them in big cities (17). The most important route into this hinterland is along the river Rhine.

Photograph (18) shows the city centre which was built again after it was bombed in the second world war. The oldest docks in the port are in the background.

Cargoes come from all parts of the world. Oil from the North Sea and Saudi Arabia arrives in oil tankers. The port is packed with oil storage tanks, refineries, chemical works and factories making plastics, fertilizers, rubber, detergents and many other things from oil. Half the oil is sent to other countries in small tankers and down pipelines. The longest pipeline goes to Frankfurt in West Germany over 431 kilometres away.

Bulk carrier ships bring iron ore (21), coal and grain to Rotterdam. Iron ore is the main cargo and this comes from as far away as Brazil and Australia

18 Rotterdam: city centre and old port area

(see map (2) on page 53). The ore is put into barges. Four barges are clamped together to make a convoy which is pushed up the river Rhine by tug (photograph (28) on page 63). The iron ore is used to make steel in West Germany. Coal comes back down the river to Rotterdam from West Germany. Most of this coal goes to steelworks in Italy, France and Britain.

There is a lot of trade between Europe and America. Much of this trade is carried in box-like containers on big container ships. Small container ships carry containers from Rotterdam to Britain. Another million containers are carried to and from the port every year on lorries which go to all parts of Europe.

FOLLOW-UP WORK

1 Use map (17) and an atlas for these questions.
   (a) Why do you think Rotterdam is often called the 'gateway to Europe'?
   (b) Name the countries and cities inside the 500 kilometre circle drawn round Rotterdam. The first letter of each name is shown on the map.
   (c) Why do factories in West Germany use the port of Rotterdam which is in the Netherlands?
   (d) Why are containers from the USA unloaded in Rotterdam before going to Britain?

17 500 kilometres around Rotterdam

2 Use map (23) on page 62 to answer these questions.
  (a) How long is the port area from the old docks to the North Sea? Give your answer in kilometres.
  (b) (i) In which direction has the port grown?
      (ii) Give two reasons for this. Think about depth of water, size of ships and space for building.
  (c) Which product uses most space at the port?
3 Study photograph (22) and map (23) on page 62.
  (a) Which two port areas are shown in the photograph?
  (b) Name the canals lettered A and B on the photograph. What type of vessel is using each canal?
  (c) What products are loaded and unloaded at sites C, D and E?
  (d) What type of sea transport is shown at site F on the photograph?
  (e) (i) Name the type of factory at G and H.
      (ii) Why is this a good place for these factories?
4 In 1944, during the second world war, all the quays on the south bank of the river were destroyed. Table (19) shows how the port has grown since the war.
  (a) Draw a line graph to show the cargo handled at the port each year between 1946 and 1981. Use a vertical scale of 1 cm to 20 million tonnes of cargo handled and a horizontal scale of 1 cm for four years.
  (b) In which ten-year period did trade grow the most?

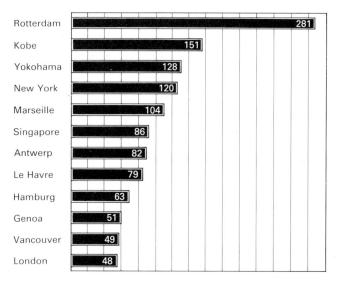

20 The world's largest ports (1980)

  (c) Which two port areas were built at that time?
  (d) How can you tell from the figures that larger ships were using the port in 1980 than in 1950?
5 Rotterdam has been the largest port in the world since 1962. New York had been the biggest until then. Graph (20) shows Rotterdam is now very big. About how many times bigger (as shown by cargo handled) is Rotterdam than:
  (a) New York;
  (b) London?

21 Unloading iron ore from a bulk carrier in Europoort

19 Ships and cargo in Rotterdam

Year	Number of ships (thousands)	Cargo handled (million tonnes)
1946	4	8
1948	9	16
1950	13	30
1952	15	40
1954	18	49
1956	21	72
1958	22	74
1960	24	83
1962	26	97
1964	27	114
1966	28	130
1968	32	159
1970	32	226
1972	33	268
1974	33	282
1976	32	288
1978	31	269
1980	30	281
1981	29	251

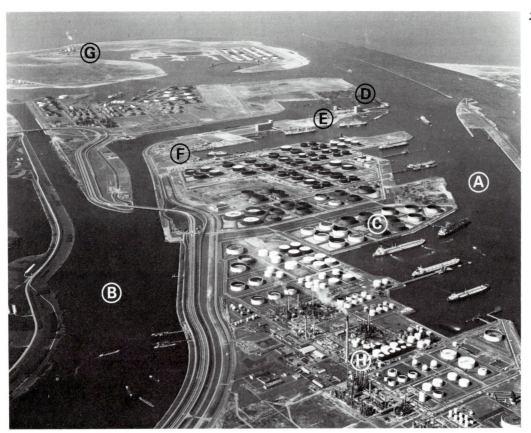

23 Map of port

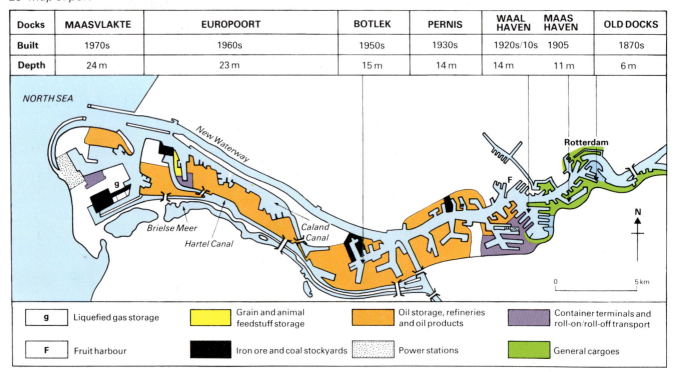

Docks	MAASVLAKTE	EUROPOORT	BOTLEK	PERNIS	WAAL HAVEN	MAAS HAVEN	OLD DOCKS
Built	1970s	1960s	1950s	1930s	1920s/10s	1905	1870s
Depth	24 m	23 m	15 m	14 m	14 m	11 m	6 m

g	Liquefied gas storage
F	Fruit harbour

Grain and animal feedstuff storage

Iron ore and coal stockyards

Oil storage, refineries and oil products

Power stations

Container terminals and roll-on/roll-off transport

General cargoes

6 Oil tankers, bulk carriers and container ships visit the port every day (25, 26, 27).
   (a) How can you tell the use for each of these ships by its design? Draw and colour sketches of these ships.
   (b) Where on photograph (22) can each ship dock? Give a letter for each answer.
   (c) How do the pictures of these ships help you with question 4(d)?

7 Draw a column graph to show the types of cargo loaded and unloaded in the port of Rotterdam in 1981. Use the figures in table (24) and a vertical scale of 1 cm to 10 per cent of cargo handled. How much of the cargo handled is crude oil and iron ore?

24 *Types of cargo handled in Rotterdam (1981) (by volume)*

Type of cargo	% of total
Crude oil (petroleum)	36
Iron ore	14
Petroleum products	10
Animal foodstuffs	6
Coal	5
Chemical products, e.g. acids	5
Steel, steel products, vehicles and machines	3
Vegetable oils and fat	3
Cereals	2
Fertilizers	2
Others	14

25 Container ship

26 Oil tanker

27 Bulk carrier

8 Photograph (28) shows a push-tow convoy taking iron ore to the steelworks of the Ruhr in West Germany.
  (a) *Each* barge carries 2000 tonnes of ore. How many journeys will it take this *convoy* to carry a shipload of 80 000 tonnes of ore up river?
  (b) Draw a sketch of the scene. Label the barges, push-tug and river Rhine.
  (c) Why is the river a good way to carry iron ore to the Ruhr?
9 Look at table (29).
  (a) Why does more traffic go upstream than downstream?
  (b) Why does crude oil *not* go by barge?
  (c) Why is coal a cargo up *and* down the Rhine?
  (d) Why are there more manufactured things coming downstream than going upstream?

28 Push-tow convoy

29 *Goods traffic on the Rhine to and from Rotterdam (1981)*

Upstream	million tonnes
Iron ore	28
Petroleum products	9
Coal (mainly steam coal for power stations)	3
Animal foodstuffs	3
Other metal ores	2
Vegetable oils and fats	2
Fertilizers	2
Chemicals	1
Cereals	1
Others, e.g. wood, salt, sand	6
Total	57

Downstream	million tonnes
Coal (mainly coking coal for steel works)	3
Sand, gravel, slag and stone	2
Chemicals	1
Steel sheets, pipes, bars, etc.	1
Others, e.g. cement, machinery, motors	4
Total	11

West Germany

We have seen how Rotterdam is a port for West Germany. This is an industrial country like Britain.

In 1933 Adolf Hitler came to power in Germany. He wanted to control all of Europe. His army attacked Poland in 1939 and this started the second world war. It lasted for five and a half years and 55 million people died: Germany was defeated. On 30th April 1945 Hitler killed himself and eight days later the war was over. Most German towns were in ruins with one-quarter of all the houses destroyed and most roads, railways and bridges smashed (2). The four Allied Powers – Great Britain, the USA, France and the USSR – in victory took control of Germany in four zones. Land east of the rivers Oder and Neisse was added to Poland (1). In 1949 the British, French and American zones were put together to make the Federal Republic of Germany (West Germany) and the Russian zone became the

2 Cologne: war damaged city

German Democratic Republic (East Germany). The German people are now in two countries. The boundary between them is the line where British, French and American armies moving in from the west met the Russian army from the east, at the end of the war. Cities in West Germany were built again (3) and new factories opened.

1 Germany: East and West

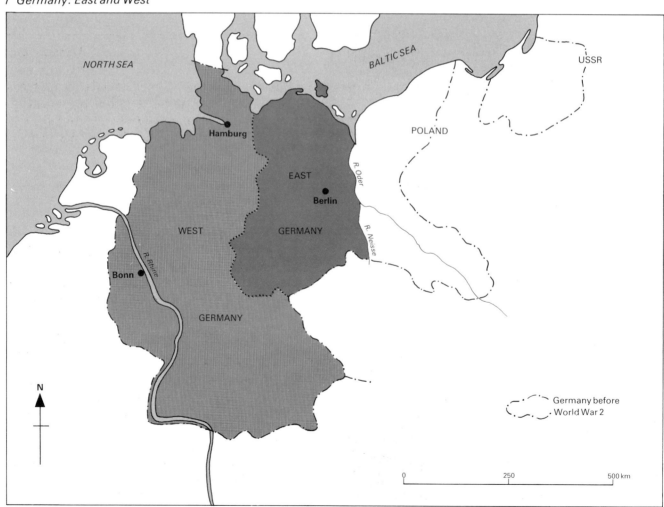

64

3 Cologne: rebuilt city

Map (4) shows West Germany has many countries around it. A lot of its exports go to them. Look how the Rhine links the mountains, uplands and lowlands of Germany as it flows northwards. The river valley has been used as a routeway for

5 Rhine: industry at Duisburg

6 Rhine: a few kilometres upstream

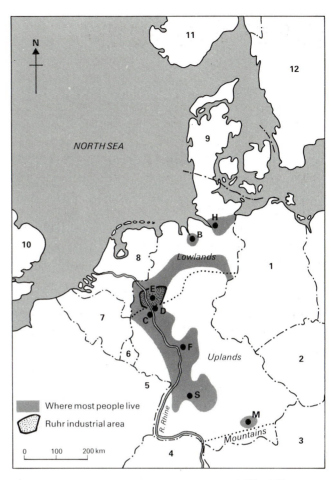

4 West Germany

thousands of years. The Romans used it to reach the far corners of their empire, including Britain. Now the river is busier than ever before. Motorways and railways follow the valley and big cities have grown up along it.

FOLLOW-UP WORK

1 Why are there two Germanies?
2 Copy map (4). Use an atlas to complete it like this.
   (a) Name the countries numbered from 1 to 12.
   (b) Name the cities. The first letter is shown for each city.
3 (a) Look at your map. Why has West Germany a good location for trading with many countries in Europe?
   (b) West Germany trades most with France and the Netherlands. Give some reasons for this.
4 (a) Why does the river Rhine flow northwards?
   (b) Why are there a lot of towns and cities along the river Rhine?
   (c) Draw sketches of the scenes in photographs (5) and (6). Label any uses for the river and the land near to the river that you can see.

Industry on the Ruhr coalfield

The push-tow convoy coming up the Rhine from Rotterdam (page 63) is taking iron ore to Duisburg. After Rotterdam this is the busiest port on the river. More steel is made here than anywhere else in Europe. Photograph (8) shows the harbour at Duisburg. Here are all the materials needed to make steel in the nearby steel works. The coal comes from local mines (9) between the rivers Emscher and Lippe (7). This is the biggest coal field in Europe. Oil comes up the pipeline from Rotterdam. Limestone is brought from the hills south of the river Ruhr.

There is another steel works on the Rhine at Rheinhausen (7). Dortmund is the next biggest steel town after Duisburg. Iron ore for these steel works comes from Sweden. The underground mine at Kiruna in northern Sweden is shown in photograph (10). The iron ore comes by ship to the West German port of Emden and then by barge along a canal to Dortmund.

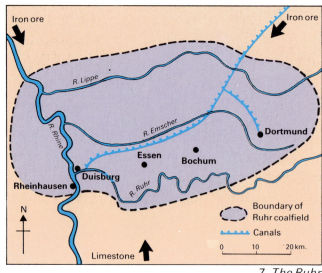

7 The Ruhr

Six million people live between Dortmund and Duisburg. It is packed with housing and factories. There is a big engineering works at Essen and a car factory at Bochum (11).

8 Harbour at Duisburg

66

9 Modern coal mine in the Ruhr

FOLLOW-UP WORK

1 Look at photograph (8). How do these things help the steel industry at Duisburg:
   (a) flat land;
   (b) river Rhine;
   (c) the Ruhr coal field;
   (d) railways and motorway;
   (e) large cities nearby?

2 Find Kiruna on a map of Europe. Trace the route of the iron ore from the ice-free port of Narvik (Norway) and from the port of Lulea to the Ruhr steel works via the ports of Rotterdam and Emden. Why is Sweden well placed to supply West Germany with iron ore?

3 Teesside has been called the Ruhr area of Britain. Look back at page 52 and answer either true or false to each of these.
   Both areas (Teesside and the Ruhr):
   (a) are near to a big river;
   (b) use local coal;
   (c) can handle big iron ore ships;
   (d) get iron ore from Sweden;
   (e) use oil from the North Sea;
   (f) use limestone from nearby hills;
   (g) use barges on canals;
   (h) send steel to local industries;
   (i) use the North Sea to get to world markets.

10 Iron ore mine in Kiruna, Sweden

4 The Ruhr area shown on map (7) was a big industrial area in the age of coal and steel. Now there are new industries. Why are cities like Duisburg and Bochum good places to have new industries like electrical, chemical and car factories?

5 Look at chart (12). Complete each part by adding the word 'increased' or 'decreased'.
   Between 1955 and 1980:
   (a) the amount of coal mined has _____;
   (b) the number of coal mines has _____;
   (c) coal output from each mine has _____;
   (d) the number of miners has _____;
   (e) coal output by each miner has _____;
   (f) the use of oil for energy has _____;
   (g) the use of coal for energy has _____;

6 (a) Give reasons for your answer to question 5(e). Use photograph (9) and your answer to 5(b) to help you.
   (b) Why will less oil be used in the future?
   (c) Why will this *help* the Ruhr coal field area?

11 Bochum car factory

12 Ruhr coal production (million tonnes)

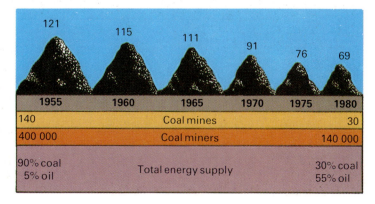

	1955	1960	1965	1970	1975	1980
	121	115	111	91	76	69
Coal mines	140					30
Coal miners	400 000					140 000
Total energy supply	90% coal 5% oil					30% coal 55% oil

The problem of pollution

The Ruhr was once farmland with a few market towns along the road going east from Duisburg. These towns grew into cities and the farmland has gone. Coal mines, steel works, power stations, chemical works, engineering factories, motorways, railways and canals have changed the scenery (13). We saw this happen in Britain (page 22). There used to be fresh air to breathe, clean water to drink and countryside to enjoy. Now any open spaces in a city are next to factories (14) which fill the air with dust, smoke and gas. It would be risky to scoop up a handful of water from a stream to drink. The water might be filled with sewage, hot water from power stations and chemicals from factories. The Rhine, for example, is now twenty times more polluted than it was in 1950. There are 2000 different chemicals mixed in the water. Chemical works on the river banks pour waste acids into it. Rotterdam

13 *Industrial landscape in Essen*

also pollutes the river and the air (15). Read the newspaper items (16). Pollution damages and kills all living things, including people.

16 *Newspaper items*

14 *Steel works and park in Dortmund*

Poison Gas Cloud   September 1982

During a large fire at the K. Chemical Factory of Cologne on Wednesday, a gas cloud formed which at times threatened the inhabitants. The fire department reports that the population were asked via loudspeaker announcements and radio spots to keep doors and windows closed and remain in their homes.

Rhine Poisoned by Chemicals   October 1982

Since Friday, Amsterdam and the Province of North Holland can no longer use water from the Rhine as drinking water. The Dutch waterworks have stopped the use of Rhine water until further notice, following the discovery of strong pollution by toxic chemicals near Lobith at the Dutch border.

15 *Rotterdam pollutes the air*

FOLLOW-UP WORK

1 Say how each of these can cause pollution:
(a) houses;
(b) cars and lorries;
(c) ships entering Rotterdam harbour;
(d) coal mining;
(e) chemical works;
(f) coal- and oil-fired power stations.

2 Say how each of these can be damaged and killed by pollution:
(a) trees;
(b) fish;
(c) people.

3 Copy map (17) of the Rhine and the rivers that flow into it (its tributaries). Colour sections of the river like this.
L little pollution – blue
M moderate pollution – orange
H heavy pollution – red
Dots on the river show a change in the amount of pollution.
   With the help of your map say why:
(a) the upper parts of tributary rivers near their sources are cleaner than the lower parts where they enter the Rhine;
(b) the most polluted water is in the industrial areas;
(c) the river Emscher is more polluted than the river Ruhr;
(d) the Rhine in Switzerland is cleaner than the Rhine in the Netherlands;
(e) the factories of West Germany cause pollution in the North Sea;
(f) the help of four countries is needed to make the Rhine a clean river.

4 Factories have tall chimneys so that fumes can be carried away in the wind. Power stations have tall cooling towers. These spread pollution from one country to another as you can see in diagram (18). Britain also adds pollution to the air which reaches Norway and Sweden by the wind. Copy diagram (18) and add these notes in the correct place.
   Sulphur fumes from factories in the Ruhr / Mix with water vapour from power stations to form

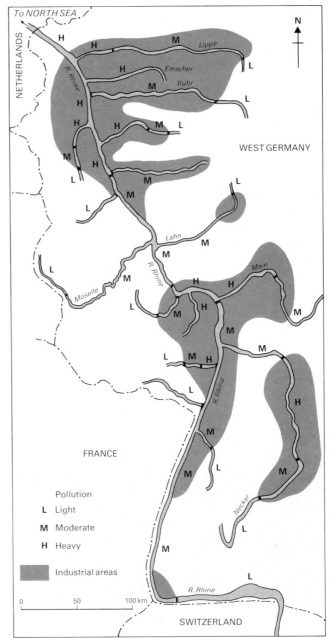

17 Pollution of the Rhine in West Germany

sulphuric acid / South-west winds carry the acid water droplets to Sweden / The air rises, cools and acid rain falls / Lakes and streams are polluted and forests die.

18 The spread of pollution

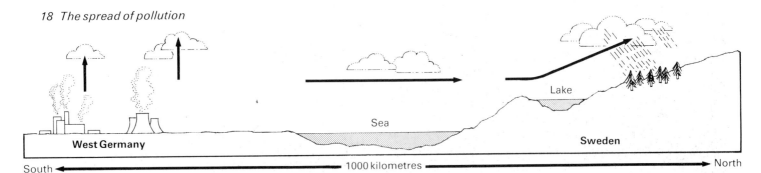

New industries

Computers: the importance of people

In your study of industry on Teesside and in West Germany you have seen how important it is to get raw materials. Steel works are built where iron ore, coal, oil and limestone can be brought together cheaply (page 52 and 66). Oil refineries are dotted around the coast (page 51) where oil arrives from the North Sea and from other countries.

When we look at new industries like making computers we find people are more important than materials. The industry needs their ideas and skills (1, 2).

1 Making up circuits for a computer

2 Inside a factory making computers at Dunstable

Factories are built where people live and where computers are needed, not where raw materials are located or gathered together. The parts for a computer are small, light and valuable, and can be moved easily by road or aeroplane. Electricity for the factory can be taken from the power supply in any town or city in Britain.

The world's biggest maker of computers is International Business Machines (IBM). This company started making office tabulating machines in America in 1904. As trade grew they opened factories in other countries. Computers have now taken the place of tabulating machines. IBM built a factory in Greenock, Scotland, in 1951 (5, 6). The government wanted the factory here to give jobs to unemployed people from the shipyards. Another factory was built in 1966 at Havant on the south coast of England. It was put here because it was next to a research centre (4, 5) where there were many

3 Computers in use

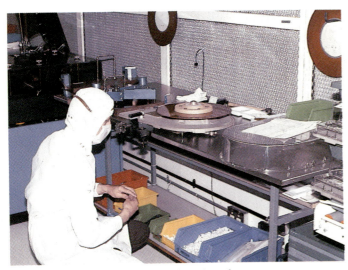

4 *Research on computers in a dust-free room*

skilled people. In 1984 the company employed 15 000 people in Britain. The Havant factory makes medium-sized computers and bases for chips (7). The Greenock factory makes visual display units and puts chips onto cards.

The chips come from an IBM factory in France and the cards from West Germany. Each chip costs £40 and a card (10 cm × 5 cm) of chips costs £1,000. The cards are sent to IBM's thirteen factories in Europe which make computers.

New ideas lead to new products. One type of office computer is replaced by a new model every five years. The people who make and sell them must learn all about the new machine at one of the company's education centres. For every one person who makes the computer there are four people working on new ideas, making programs, making decisions and selling the goods. As you can see, people are very important in this industry.

7 *Experimental chip*

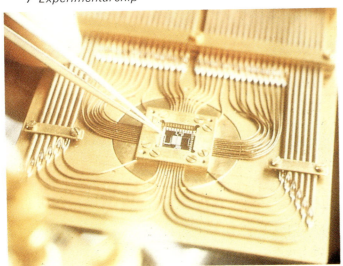

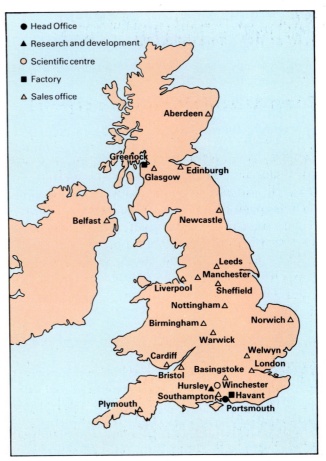

5 *IBM in Britain*

6 *IBM factory in Greenock*

A YEAR OF DECISIONS AT THE COMPANY

Work in small groups. Imagine that you are the board of directors of IBM. The board has to discuss many things. Write down what you would do and your reasons.

1 The company has spent a lot of money in the research laboratory working on a new computer. A Japanese company has made a similar model, ahead of you and at a lower cost than you wanted to charge. Should you:
   (a) scrap the project (the cost of a new assembly line will cost millions of pounds);
   (b) re-design the computer to include more features and be at a lower price;
   (c) do a survey to find out if you can sell your computer to enough customers to cover the cost of making it?

2 You need a new plastic component (part) for a computer to be made at Greenock. Should you:
   (a) buy the component from a local supplier if the price is reasonable;
   (b) buy at the lowest price possible in Britain;
   (c) buy at the lowest price possible in Europe?

3 Fewer people are now buying the electric typewriter made at one of your factories. Should you:
   (a) lay-off workers at the factory;
   (b) move some of the workers to another factory and still make some typewriters at the factory;
   (c) choose this factory for your new computer and make fewer typewriters? (Other IBM factories want to make the new computer.)

4 Your company has a worldwide market for computers. More workers are needed. Should you:
   (a) move up people in your own company and train young school leavers to fill their places;
   (b) get skilled workers and managers from other companies by offering high wages;
   (c) bring in people from places where there is unemployment?

5 You want to sell more computers. You can:
   (a) advertise on television;
   (b) use direct selling methods contacting people by letter and telephone;
   (c) advertise in newspapers and magazines;
   (d) have a computer exhibition;
   (e) open more shops and sales offices.
   Which methods will you use to sell:
      (i) more small computers;
      (ii) more large (mainframe) computers (8)?

6 The British government want a new computer system at the lowest price for their tax offices. Other companies in Britain, Europe, America and Japan want to make it. Should you:
   (a) offer to make the computer for a very small profit to win the order;
   (b) show the government that your computer is the best and try to get a good profit;
   (c) ignore this contract and look for orders with a higher profit?

7 The Italian government wants you to build another factory in Italy, where business is booming. Should you:
   (a) make your factory in northern Italy bigger (you sell a lot of computers there);
   (b) build a new factory in Rome, the capital city;
   (c) build a new factory in southern Italy where there are a lot of poor people and unemployment? The government will give you land and money to build in the south.

8 You now have many factories in Europe. Should *each* factory:
   (a) make one product and sell this all over Europe;
   (b) make two or three products and sell them all over Europe;
   (c) make a lot of products and sell all of them in the home country?

9 You have money to spend in the community to show you are a caring citizen and to get publicity. You can sponsor only three projects this year from these requests:
   (a) youth workshop – huts and help to make craft products;
   (b) river clean-up and tree-planting campaign;
   (c) tennis tournament;
   (d) Chichester Theatre;
   (e) nautical museum;
   (f) a school swimming pool;
   (g) a community hall;
   (h) computer centre for schools.
   Which will you choose?

8 Large mainframe computer

Electronics and the way we live

Computers are just one part of the electronics industry. This industry also makes telecommunications equipment, radio, radar, navigational equipment, electronic instruments and equipment for ships, aircraft, space satellites, factories, hospitals, schools and homes. The industry is growing very quickly. Look at photograph (9) which shows one of the first electronic computers in 1950. It is a mass of wires and valves. In the 1950s transistors took the place of valves. Soon people were wearing transistor hearing aids and using transistor radios. In the 1960s transistors and circuits were miniaturised (made very small) and put into the surface of a

9 Early computers filled a big room

wafer of silicon called a chip. The work done by a computer which filled a room in 1950 (9) can now be done using a chip just 5 millimetres square (7). This advance means we can now have digital watches, pocket calculators, electronic games and home computers. Table (10) shows some more uses of electronics.

10 Uses for electronics

1 Air traffic control	17 Personal computer
2 Bank cash dispenser	18 Petrol pump dispenser
3 Business dictating machine	19 Robot welders
4 Car assembly line control	20 Sewing machine stitch selector
5 Car park ticket machine	21 Space flights and satellites
6 Cash register	22 Steelmaking process control
7 Central heating controls	23 Television remote control
8 Cooker controls	
9 Electronic games	24 Traffic light signals
10 Electronic organ	25 Underground railway traffic control
11 Fire and ambulance control rooms	26 Video recording machine
12 Medical monitoring equipment	27 Washing machine program selector
13 Microwave oven	28 Weighing machine
14 Motorway warning signals	29 Word processor for business letters
15 Navigation equipment	30 X-ray body scanner
16 Pay phone	

FOLLOW-UP WORK

1 The list of uses for electronics (10) is in alphabetical order. Make your own lists under these headings:
   (a) in the home;
   (b) at the office;
   (c) in a factory;
   (d) travel and transport;
   (e) at a hospital;
   (f) in the town;
   (g) at the shops.

2 Photograph (11) is a montage of different pictures showing many of the uses for electronics. Make a montage of your own using pictures from magazines. This can be a general display or based on one of your lists.

3 Use your lists and montage to help you write an essay with the title 'Electronics in our lives'.

11 Electronics in our lives

The car industry

Electronics and computers are now used to make cars. Robots (1) weld steel panels into a body shell, spray paint and fit windscreens. Computers control the assembly of thousands of parts, known as components, which make up a car. Photograph (2) shows the engine meeting its body and photograph (3) the exhaust being fitted underneath. These are two stages in a two-kilometre-long computer-controlled assembly line. You can see how a lot of cars are being made at the same time. This is called mass production.

1 Robots in a car factory

2 The engine meets the car body

3 Fitting the exhaust

The first moving assembly line to make cars was set up by Henry Ford in America in 1913. He wanted to make a simple car in large numbers for a low cost. Until then cars were made one at a time. The foundation was the chassis. Parts were brought to mechanics who built up the car on the spot. Henry Ford changed all that. He machine-made standard parts in large numbers. These were fitted to the chassis as they moved along on conveyors. Soon the Model T Ford was coming off the assembly line at the rate of one every ten seconds and two million a year. Cars are still made in the same way but now with the help of robots and computers.

Four large companies assemble cars in Britain. Their factories are in or near to London, Luton (4), Oxford, Birmingham, Coventry and Liverpool. Parts are made in two thousand factories all over Britain. Computers are used to plan the ordering and delivery of these parts to the car factories. Table

4 Car factory in Luton

(5) shows where Vauxhall car factory in Luton gets its components. Many parts come from Europe. In 1925 Vauxhall Motors became part of General Motors. This American company is the biggest car maker in the world. General Motors makes cars in Britain, West Germany (see page 67), Belgium, Portugal and Spain.

The same car models are made in Britain and in Europe. This means that one factory can make components, such as petrol tanks, for all the cars in all the factories. Britain makes some of these parts and imports others.

Things have changed since the first Vauxhall car was made in 1903. It was a five-horse power one-cylinder car (6) which could reach a speed of 25 m.p.h. It had wire wheels, tiller steering and no reverse gear. Forty were sold at a price of £136 each.

The car is now the most popular way to travel. There are 15 million cars on the roads in Britain. Of all the journeys people take, only 10 per cent are by bus or coach, 7 per cent by rail and less than 1 per cent by air. Eighty per cent of all freight goes by road in two million lorries. Motorways (7) are made for high speed travel. There are three thousand kilometres of motorway in Britain and they carry one quarter of the heavy lorries. Photograph (8) shows cars on a transporter heading for London along the M1 motorway.

6 The first Vauxhall car 1903

5 Components for the car factory at Luton

Component	Suppliers from Britain	Suppliers from Europe
Sheet steel	Wales, Scotland	West Germany, Belgium, Netherlands
Castings, forgings and alloy steels	Sheffield	nil
Paint	West Midlands	Belgium
Wheels	West Midlands	West Germany, Italy, Switzerland
Tyres	Midlands	nil
Radiators	Yorkshire	France
Gearboxes	Lancashire, West Midlands	West Germany
Petrol tanks	nil	Netherlands
Exhaust systems	Lancashire, Wales	West Germany
Bumpers	West Midlands, London area	nil
Batteries	London area	France
Electrics	West Midlands, London area	West Germany
Glass	West Midlands	West Germany, Italy, Finland
Upholstery and carpets	West Yorkshire	nil

7 Traffic on the M1 motorway

8 Car transporter on the motorway

CAR MAKERS

This is a game for two or three players. Each player is a car maker with the job of assembling at their factory components made in many parts of Britain. Ask your teacher for the things you need to play the game.

How to play the game

1 **Fact.** Cars are made in London, Luton, Oxford, Coventry, Birmingham and Liverpool.
   Game. Each player chooses one of these places to make cars. Each of these places is marked by a big circle on the board map.

2 **Fact.** Components are made in all the towns and cities shown on the game board map. Photographs (9), (10), (11), (12) and (13) show some of these components. Computers are used to plan the supply of components to the car assembly works.
   Game. Each player takes a supply card from the pack. If two towns make the component the player chooses one of them to supply the factory. A counter is placed on the town (shown by a small circle) which is chosen.

3 **Fact.** Components are carried by the component-maker's own lorries to the car works. The fastest journeys are on the motorways. There may be delays and hazards along the way.
   Game. Each player in turn throws the dice. On a throw of 1, 2, 3, 4 and 5 the counter is moved the correct number of spaces by road *from* the town where it is made *towards* that player's car works. Care must be taken in choosing a route. If a 6 is thrown, a hazard card is drawn from the pack, the instructions carried out and the card returned to the bottom of the pack.

4 **Fact.** At the car works, sheet steel is cut to size,

9 *Making cloth for car seats in Manchester*

pressed into shapes and welded together to make car bodies. Components are added as the body moves along the assembly line.

Game. When a component (counter) arrives at the car-making town it is placed into the car body shown on the board for that player. If the component is made in the town where the car works is located the counter is placed directly onto the car body. This player does not throw the dice because transport is not needed.

When a component reaches the car works another card is drawn from the supply pack and another counter brought into play.

The first player to make a car with eight components wins the game.

10 *Making rear lamps in Cannock*

11 *Making glass in St Helens*

12 Making clutches in Leamington Spa

FOLLOW-UP WORK

1 Look at the first Vauxhall car (6) on page 75 and at cars now being made (page 74). Write a few sentences about how cars have changed and how this has changed our lives.
2 Look at the photographs of the motorways (7, 8) on page 75. List the reasons why cars and lorries can travel faster on motorways than on other roads.
3 Why are cars made on an assembly line?
4 Look at photographs (9, 10, 11, 12) of components being made. In what way is the making of components different from making a car?
5 Why do American companies like Ford and General Motors make cars in Britain and in Europe?

13 Engines being assembled in London

6 Why do people in Britain buy cars made in other countries instead of cars made in Britain? Give a few reasons.
7 Fifteen million vehicles are made in Europe every year. Table (14) shows how many are made in Britain.
   (a) Draw a line graph using a scale on the vertical axis of 1 cm for 200 000 vehicles. What does the graph show?
   (b) Why does making more cars help Britain?

14 Vehicles made in Britain

Year	Millions
1973	2.2
1974	1.9
1975	1.6
1976	1.7
1977	1.7
1978	1.6
1979	1.5
1980	1.3
1981	1.2
1982	1.1

If you played the game answer these questions.
8   (a) Where was your car factory?
     (b) Why did you choose it? Would you choose a different place next time? Say why.
9   Why is it wise to have:
     (a) more than one supplier of each component;
     (b) one company making many components for your car works?
10   Use the scale on the game board map to do this question.
     (a) Measure in kilometres the longest journey you made.
     (b) If the lorry travelled at 80 km per hour on the motorways and 40 km per hour on the other roads, how long did this journey take?
     (c) Which of these two journeys would be done quickest:
        Leeds to London, or
        Plymouth to London?
11   The next stage of the game would be to sell the cars you have made. Is your car works in a good location to:
     (a) sell cars in Britain;
     (b) export cars to Europe or America?
     Say why.

RESEARCH

Steel is just one of the materials which are used to make a car. Name some more and find out how and where they are made.

London

In 1801 ten million people lived in Britain. By 1901 the number had grown to 37 million. Most of these extra people lived in towns and cities. The building of factories caused more people to move into towns and cities from the countryside. London grew faster than any other city. In 1881 four million people lived there and by 1941 there were eight million.

Even though many people have now moved to towns outside London, one-eighth of the people of Britain still live there. It is the largest city and the capital city of the United Kingdom. A view over the centre of the city (1) shows that a lot of people now work in offices. This is many more than work in factories in London.

Twelve million people from all over Britain visit London every year. One-third of them have business to do and the others come to see the sights or to visit friends and relatives. Another eight million visitors come from abroad, mainly from America, West Germany, France and the Netherlands. One-fifth of them come on business and the others come on holiday. So you can see London is a very busy place.

A VISIT TO LONDON

Your pen-friend in Paris is coming to stay with you for the summer holidays. You can stay three days in London with two nights at an hotel. Your friend has sent a list of interesting places (4) but wants you to plan the visit.

1 Choose seven places from the list which you would like to visit. Find the seven places on the map of London (5).

2 Tower of London

1 Offices in central London

2 Choose an hotel for your stay.
3 Plan each day of your visit.
   (a) Choose two places to visit on day 1, three places for day 2 and two places for day 3.
   (b) Plan out the route you will take each day from your hotel.
   You will get around London on the underground railway and by walking. You can have a trip on the river Thames.
4 The cost of your train journey to London and two-night stay in an hotel depends on the distance you have to travel and the category of the hotel you have chosen. Use map (6) and table (7) on page 80 to work these out.
   (a) How much would your visit to London cost at these 1984 prices?

3 Trafalgar Square

(b) How much more would it cost a person going to London from Grampian than a person travelling from Kent?

5 Look at map (8) which shows fast train times to London.

(a) At what time will you need to set off from *your* nearest railway station to arrive in London by 12 noon?

(b) At which railway station will you arrive in London?

(c) Are you still happy with the hotel you chose? Why?

4 Interesting places to visit

1 **British Museum** Museum of history, archaeology and art
2 **Buckingham Palace** London home of the Sovereign
3 **Downing Street No 10** is the official home of the Prime Minister
4 **Horse Guards** Mounted sentries of the Household Cavalry, Life Guards and Blues and Royals
5 **Houses of Parliament** Centre of government. House of Lords and House of Commons. Big Ben is the bell in the clock tower
6 **London Zoo** Many of the 6000 animals are kept in open areas in Regent's Park
7 **Madame Tussauds** Wax figures of famous and notorious people
8 **Marble Arch and Hyde Park** Triumphal arch near the entrance to the Royal Park
9 **Museum of London** The history of London from earliest times to the present day
10 **National Gallery** Art gallery with the best paintings of many European artists
11 **Natural History Museum** Rooms with models and fossils of dinosaurs and huge mammals

12 **Oxford Street** Famous shopping street with large stores
13 **Science Museum** The history of science and industry with working models and displays
14 **St Paul's Cathedral** Sir Christopher Wren's famous city church with great dome and Whispering Gallery
15 **Stock Exchange** Buying and selling stocks and shares can be viewed from a gallery
16 **Tower Bridge** Drawbridge across the river Thames built in 1894
17 **Tower of London** (2) The White Tower was built for William the Conqueror in 1078. Once a fortress, palace and prison. Stronghold for the Crown Jewels
18 **Trafalgar Square** (3) The square with the column and statue of Nelson commemorates Lord Nelson's victory at Trafalgar in 1805
19 **Victoria and Albert Museum** World-famous art collection and sculptures
20 **Westminster Abbey** Most Sovereigns have been crowned here since the abbey was rebuilt for Edward the Confessor in 1065

5 London

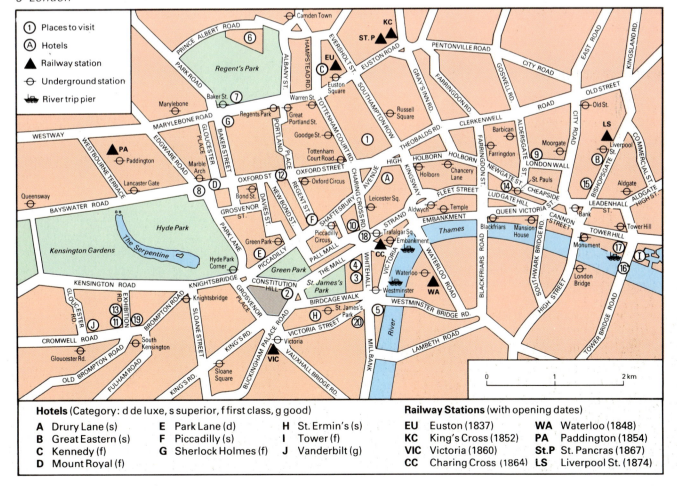

Hotels (Category: d de luxe, s superior, f first class, g good)

A	Drury Lane (s)	E	Park Lane (d)	H	St. Ermin's (s)
B	Great Eastern (s)	F	Piccadilly (s)	I	Tower (f)
C	Kennedy (f)	G	Sherlock Holmes (f)	J	Vanderbilt (g)
D	Mount Royal (f)				

Railway Stations (with opening dates)

EU	Euston (1837)	WA	Waterloo (1848)
KC	King's Cross (1852)	PA	Paddington (1854)
VIC	Victoria (1860)	St.P	St. Pancras (1867)
CC	Charing Cross (1864)	LS	Liverpool St. (1874)

(d) Trains leave Birmingham New Street, Exeter and Newcastle at 9.00 a.m. At what times *and* at which stations do they arrive in London?

(e) Which is nearest to London
  (i) in distance (see (6)),
  (ii) in time (see (8)):
  Plymouth or Newcastle;
  Sheffield or Leeds;
  Ipswich or Coventry?

(f) Copy the time chart (9). Mark a line from London in the direction of each of the towns on map (6). The length of the line is the time it takes to reach London from each town. Plymouth has been done for you.

(g) In what way is Leeds *nearer* than Sheffield to London?

(h) How do fast trains affect how far people live from their work?

6 Rail travel regions

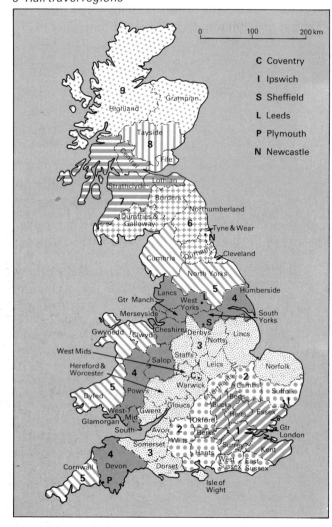

8 Fast travel times by rail to London

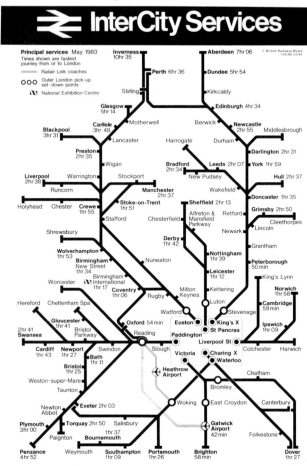

7 Cost of travel and hotel for two nights (per person)

Region	Category			
	Deluxe	Superior	First class	Good
1	£68	£56	£47	£39
2	72	59	50	43
3	75	63	54	46
4	79	67	58	50
5	84	72	63	55
6	88	76	67	59
7	92	79	70	63
8	95	83	74	66
9	98	86	77	69

9 Time chart

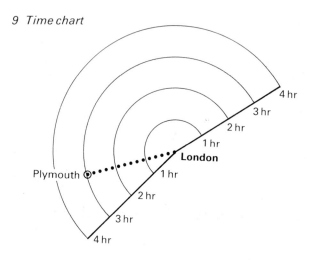

Living and working in London

Almost seven million people live in London. The City is the oldest part. This is where Roman and medieval London used to be. London grew outwards from the City. The main railway stations show where the edge of London was in the nineteenth century. These stations and their opening dates are with map (5) on page 79. More land has been used for buildings since then. In Outer London there are a lot of detached and semi-detached houses with gardens (10). You do not get these near the centre of London (11).

The one square mile of the City of London is packed with office buildings. This is the money and business centre of Britain. Here is the Bank of England and the Stock Exchange. There are also four hundred foreign banks and the offices of many insurance and trading companies. All these companies deal in money and what they do will affect people living all around the world. Perhaps they are deciding the price of tea from Kenya, to lend money to build a power station in Brazil and so on.

Banks and companies want their main offices to be near the Bank of England and the Stock Exchange. But there is very little space here so skyscrapers are needed. The tallest building in Britain is the 52-storey National Westminster Tower in Old Broad Street near the Bank of England (12). It opened in 1980. It is 183 metres high and from the top you can see the whole of London (1). The middle of the building is made from concrete. The staircases and lifts are inside it. The offices are in the three steel wings. The building weighs 140 000 tonnes and needed foundations 20 metres deep with 375 piles a further 25 metres into the London clay. The Tower is the centre of the National Westminster Bank's international banking. Two thousand five hundred people work there. Most of them live in Outer London but some travel from as far away as Luton, Colchester, Southend, Worthing, Guildford and Reading.

12 National Westminster Tower

10 Near Heathrow airport

11 Tower Hamlets

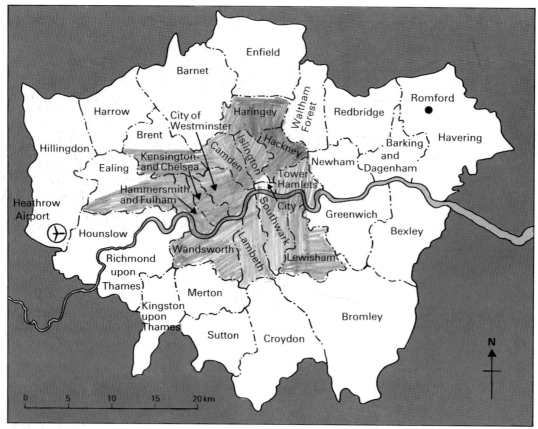

13 Greater London

14 London boroughs

Inner London boroughs	Number of people per hectare		Outer London boroughs	Number of people per hectare		Outer London boroughs	Number of people per hectare
1 Camden	79		A Barking and Dagenham	44		N Kingston upon Thames	35
2 Hackney	93		B Barnet	33		O Merton	44
3 Hammersmith and Fulham	92		C Bexley	35		P Redbridge	40
4 Haringey	67		D Brent	57		Q Richmond upon Thames	29
5 Islington	108		E Bromley	20		R Sutton	39
6 Kensington and Chelsea	116		F Croydon	37		S Waltham Forest	54
7 Lambeth	90		G Ealing	50			
8 Lewisham	67		H Enfield	32		City of London	21
9 Newham	58		I Greenwich	45			
10 Southwark	74		J Harrow	39			
11 Tower Hamlets	72		K Havering	20			
12 Wandsworth	73		L Hillingdon	21			
13 City of Westminster	89		M Hounslow	34			

FOLLOW-UP WORK

Use map (13) and table (14) to do these.

1 What is the distance from Heathrow airport to
   (a) the City,
   (b) Romford?

2 Is the area of Greater London 500 km², 1500 km², 3000 km² or 4500 km²?

3 Copy map (13). Colour each borough like this:

Fewer than 40 people per hectare – green
40 to 69 people per hectare – brown
70 or more people per hectare – red

4 (a) What is the pattern on your map and what does it show?
   (b) Do more people live in the older or newer parts of London? Say why.

5 Draw the housing shown in photographs (10) and (11) on page 81.

82

6 What would you like and dislike about living:
   (a) in Tower Hamlets;
   (b) near Heathrow airport?
   Mention the houses, environment, jobs, travel to work, and any other things you know.
7 (a) Why do banks want an office near to the centre of London?
   (b) Why do people live a long way from the offices where they work?
8 (a) The cost of renting offices is highest when a lot of companies want them near the City centre. Copy graph (15) which is a cross-section of the City. Colour the columns to the correct height using the figures in table (16).
   (b) What does your graph show?
9 A million people travel into the centre of London each weekday morning. They are called commuters. It may take them an hour or more to get to work. They work in offices, shops,

17 Road traffic in London

restaurants, hotels, theatres, cinemas, on the buses and on the underground. The streets are full of traffic (17) and the underground trains packed with passengers (19). In the evening people go back home to the suburbs and to towns outside London.
   (a) Draw a column graph to show the type of transport people use to get to work in the centre of London. Use the percentages in table (18) and a vertical scale of 1 cm for 10 per cent of passengers
   (b) How many passengers use private transport (car and cycle) and how many use public transport (bus and train)?
   (c) How many types of vehicles can you see on the roads in London (17)? Name them.
   (d) Why do buses cause less traffic congestion than if everyone used cars?
   (e) Draw a line graph like this. Use a scale of 1 cm for 20 000 passengers on the vertical axis and of 1 cm for each hour from 07:00 to 22:00 hours on the horizontal axis. Use the figures in table (19). Draw a red line for passengers starting journeys at central London stations, a green line for passengers at suburban stations, and a black line for the total.

15 Cross-section of the City

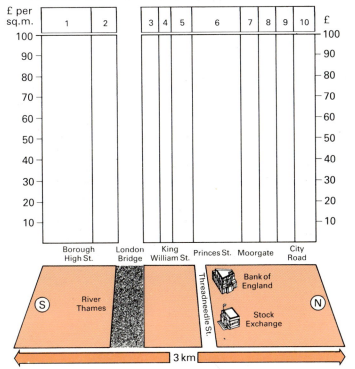

16 Office rents

Area	£ per sq. metre per year
1	30
2	40
3	60
4	75
5	90
6	100
7	90
8	70
9	60
10	45

18 Going to work

Passengers entering central London between 07.00 and 10.00 daily in 1982

Total passengers 1 023 000

Type of transport used	% of total
British Railways	28
Underground railways	29
Both British Railways and the underground	10
Car	19
Bus	10
Motor/pedal cycles	4

(f) Look at the black line graph. When are the rush hours (peak travel hours)?

(g) Look at the red and green graphs. How can you tell that people are going from the suburbs to central London and back again?

10 (a) Use a map of England to find the towns from which people travel to work at the National Westminster Tower. Which two towns are the furthest from central London?

(b) Would you like to be a commuter? Why?

(c) How can a company, like the National Westminster Bank, help their workers to miss the 'rush hour' traffic?

19 Passengers on the underground 07:00–22:00 hours

| | Passengers (in thousands) starting journeys in | | |
Hour	Central London stations	Suburban stations	Total all stations
07:00–08:00	28	103	131
08:00–09:00	106	239	345
09:00–10:00	87	80	167
10:00–11:00	48	21	69
11:00–12:00	45	14	59
12:00–13:00	57	19	76
13:00–14:00	60	22	82
14:00–15:00	55	18	73
15:00–16:00	69	23	92
16:00–17:00	135	61	196
17:00–18:00	262	76	338
18:00–19:00	102	30	132
19:00–20:00	43	21	64
20:00–21:00	31	15	46
21:00–22:00	24	13	37

Dockland

For almost 2000 years since Roman times London has been a busy port. For centuries ships docked on the north bank of the Thames in the Pool of London in the middle of the City (21). In the nineteenth century Britain was the wealthiest industrial country in the world and London the biggest port. Railways from London went to all parts of Britain.

Wealthy people built docks in the London clay. A hospital, church and 1250 houses were knocked down and 11 000 people made homeless to build St Katharine's dock next to the City. Ships could be loaded and unloaded at any state of the tide in these new docks. Big warehouses were built and dockside industries set up to use raw materials imported from all over the world. The year when each new dock opened is shown on map (21). Now look again at the photograph (16) on page 59. See how many docks you can spot.

20 Tilbury docks

21 Dockland

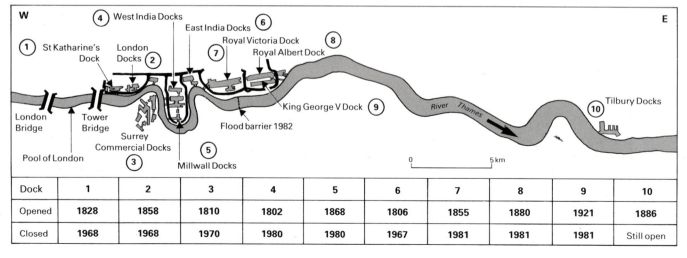

Dock	1	2	3	4	5	6	7	8	9	10
Opened	1828	1858	1810	1802	1868	1806	1855	1880	1921	1886
Closed	1968	1968	1970	1980	1980	1967	1981	1981	1981	Still open

84

London's old up-river docks have now closed (1981). The date when each dock closed is shown in map (21). Tilbury docks, 40 kilometres down-river from London Bridge, are the main docks now. There are also wharves ((un)loading places) for oil refineries, chemical works, cement works and factories. You can see some in photograph (16) on page 59 and there are more further down-river. This means London is still a busy port but much less so for world trade than a century ago.

The old docks had to close. Since the 1960s more cargoes have been carried in box-like containers (22). Large container ships (20), bulk carrier ships and oil tankers need deep water, special handling equipment and fast turn-around times. The old docks were too small, too far up-river, with too little storage space and poor roads. Look back to page 63 to see these ships and how Rotterdam became a bigger port than London.

22 Handling containers

When Britain joined the EEC there was more trade with Europe (23). Other ports near to Europe (24) such as Felixstowe, Harwich, Dover and Southampton took a share of this trade. London lost some trade and Liverpool, on the west coast, lost even more (25).

When London docks closed, factories based on them also closed. Thousands of people lost their jobs. In Tower Hamlets and Newham (map 13, page 82) this was one more problem to add to poor houses, poor shops, few parks and play areas, and poor roads.

23 Britain's trading partners (1981)

Exports to:	% of total	Imports from:	% of total
USA	12	USA	12
West Germany	11	West Germany	12
Netherlands	8	France	8
France	7	Netherlands	8
Ireland	6	Belgium/Lux.	5
Belgium/Lux.	4	Italy	5
Italy	3	Japan	4
Sweden	3	Norway	4
Switzerland	3	Saudi Arabia	4
Nigeria	3	Ireland	4
South Africa	2	Switzerland	3
Saudi Arabia	2	Sweden	3
Denmark	2	Canada	3
Others	34	Denmark	2
		Others	23

25 Cargo handled by Britain's ports (million tonnes)

Port	1971	1981
London	53	35
Southampton	28	20
Felixstowe	2	7
Liverpool	32	12
Sullom Voe	0	40

24 Ports for Europe

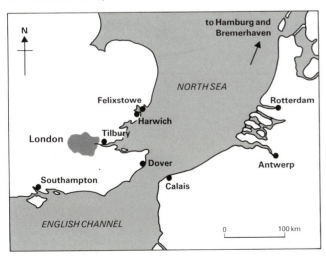

FOLLOW-UP WORK

1 Look at map (21).
   (a) In which century did most docks open?
   (b) Between which two years did docks close?
   (c) Why is Tilbury the best dock to keep open?
2 Look at map (24) and tables (23) and (25).
   (a) With which three countries of the EEC do we trade the most?
   (b) Has Liverpool or Felixstowe grown the most with trade to Europe? Say why.
   (c) Why will London always be a busy port?

New development in Dockland

3 St Katharine's dock is being used again (26). West Dock is now a yacht haven and East Dock is a museum of historic ships (28). The 826-bedroom Tower Hotel (29) and two office blocks overlook West Dock and blocks of flats overlook East Dock (30). The Ivory House warehouse has been restored (27) but now with luxury flats, tourist shops and a yacht club. Another warehouse has been made into a restaurant. An old brewery is now a restaurant and pub.

  (a) Do you think this new development *should* have

   (i) luxury flats;
   (ii) offices;
   (iii) a large hotel?

  (b) Local people wanted:

   (i) cheaper houses;
   (ii) a supermarket;
   (iii) light industries;
   (iv) a park;
   (v) a community centre;
   (vi) Ivory House kept as a working museum showing the docks as they used to be.

  What do you think about each of these ideas?

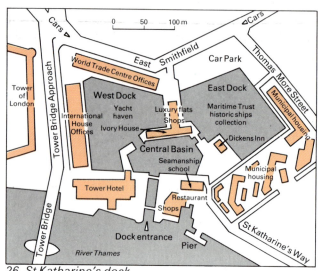

26 St Katharine's dock

28 Dock entrance, Ivory House

27 Yacht haven

29 Tower Hotel

30 Blocks of flats

4 The London Docklands Development Corporation is looking at a plan to build a mini-airport in the Royal Docks. One of these docks is shown on page 59. The runway will be between the Royal Albert Dock and King George V Dock (31). The aircraft will be quiet and use a short runway. A million passengers or 100 000 tonnes of cargo will be carried each year to cities in Britain and Europe. The airport will need 250 people and new industry might come to the area. Picture (32) shows what the airport would look like. There is also a new bridge and motorway across the Thames.

  (a) Work in small groups. Each group should elect a chairman. Your first decision is whether to have the airport in the docks.
  (b) What other developments would you have in the area? The docks must be kept as areas of water.
  (c) Copy map (31), with or without the airport. Mark in where you want your new developments.
  (d) Each chairman should talk to the class about their ideas. A vote is taken to decide the best scheme to make dockland a place where people will want to live and work.

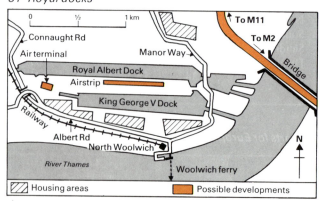

31 Royal docks

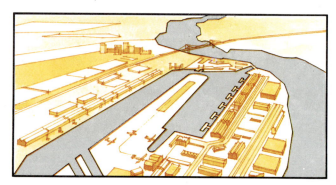

32 New development in Dockland

A new city for Britain

In the 1950s London had a lot of slum houses and run-down buildings. The city had spread over miles of lovely countryside. Slums have now been pulled down and new buildings, like blocks of flats and offices, have taken their place.

Many people have moved out of London. Some have gone to new towns (1), others live on housing estates. These are many miles from the city because some countryside is being saved. It is called the Green Belt. We have seen how people travel to work in London in the morning and back to the suburbs in the evening. A lot of time and money is spent on travel and there are big traffic jams in the rush hours.

In 1967 it was decided to build a new city called Milton Keynes half-way between London and Birmingham. People who moved from London to live there would not have to travel a long way to work because jobs would be in Milton Keynes. There would be new houses to rent or buy, a big shopping area, new schools, community centres and leisure centres.

Photograph (2) shows the site for Milton Keynes in 1970 when building began and photograph (3) is the same area in 1982 when 100 000 people lived there. Graph (4) shows where the people came from who now live there.

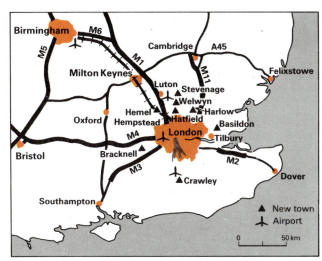

1 The location of Milton Keynes

2 Site of Milton Keynes 1970

3 Centre of Milton Keynes 1982

4 Where people came from to live in Milton Keynes

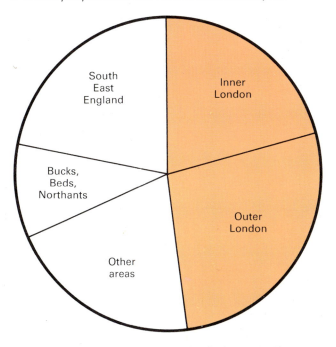

FOLLOW-UP WORK

1 Look at map (1).
   (a) Why is Milton Keynes a good place to build factories and offices?
   (b) Why will few people travel to work in London from Milton Keynes?

2 (a) Describe the land on which Milton Keynes has been built. It is shown in photograph (2).
   (b) Are there any features shown in the photograph which would be worth keeping in the new city?

3 Map (12) on page 90 shows Milton Keynes in 1984. Over 100 000 people were living there. The boundary shows the size of the city in the year 2000 when 250 000 people will live there.
   (a) Re-arrange the middle and end parts of the sentences in table (13) to make five correct statements about the plan of Milton Keynes.
   (b) The sites numbered from 1 to 4 on the map can be used for these developments: hospital, open-air stadium, the Midland and South of England soft drink distribution centre, golf course.
   Choose a site for each development. Say why you chose each site.

4 Study the photographs on page 89.
   (a) Where on map (12) is the factory?
   (b) Where are the offices and shops?
   (c) Looking at the photographs say why life in Milton Keynes is more pleasant and interesting than in many other cities.

5 The road network for Milton Keynes is a grid of one-kilometre squares with roundabouts at junctions. This is different from many cities where roads radiate like the spokes of a wheel.

Separate from the road network is Redway (6). This is a network of red asphalt paths for pedestrians and cyclists. Redway crosses the main roads by underpass or bridge and local roads at crossing points marked by yellow bollards. Study map (5) which shows north-east Milton Keynes.

Copy the network of roads. Mark onto this the routes two families living at A and B would use for these journeys.
   (a) The route the parents of family A might use to get to work at the factory by car.
   (b) The route family A might take to reach the leisure centre by car.
   Give reasons for the routes you choose.
   (c) How does the grid network of main roads help to spread traffic more evenly in the city?
   (d) Is the shortest route to the factory from B by road or Redway?
   (e) Is the shortest route from B to the leisure centre by road or Redway?
   (f) Does Redway or the main road give the shortest, most direct route?
   (g) The children walk along Redway to the nearest school.
       (i) Which family has the shortest distance to walk to school?
       (ii) Which family has a road to cross?
   (h) The children of family A and B are friends and go on cycle rides together. Plan an interesting route on Redway for them. Decide where they meet and a route of up to 10 kilometres with stops along the way. Mark the route onto your map.
   (i) Why is Redway an interesting way to get around the city?
   (j) Why is Redway good for children to use?
   (k) How does Redway help to make travel easier for motorists on the main roads?

5 *North-east Milton Keynes*

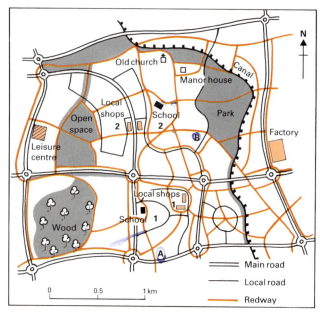

6 *Children using Redway*

7 Factory

8 Housing

9 Offices

10 Shops

11 Willen Lake Linear Park

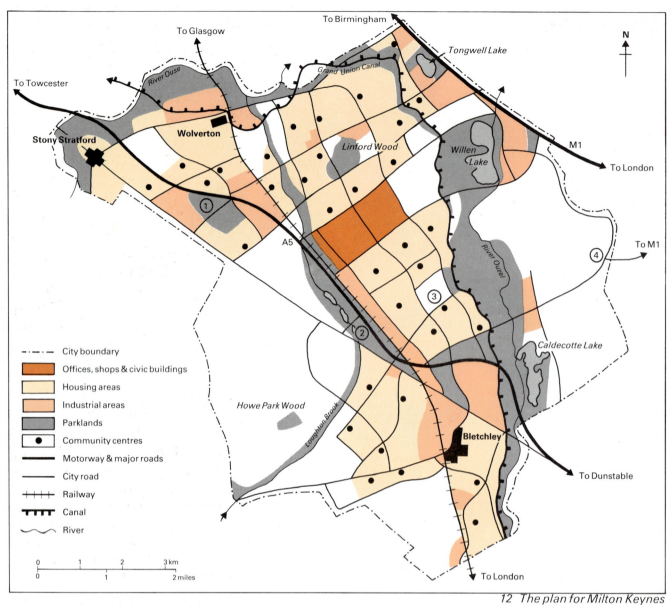

12 The plan for Milton Keynes

13 Statements about Milton Keynes

Feature		Location		Reason	
1	Offices, shops and civic buildings *1*	A	are near to the motorway and railway *3*	a	where there is water and trees *4*
2	Housing areas *2*	B	are near to the centre of the city *1*	b	so people can easily walk or cycle there *5*
3	Industrial areas *3*	C	are in a wide band down the centre of the city *2*	c	a point easily reached by car *1*
4	Parklands *4*	D	are evenly spaced within the city *5*	d	for easy assembly and distribution *3*
5	Community centres *5*	E	are along the river valleys *4*	e	so people can get to surrounding jobs and parks *2*

France

Our study of France is mainly about Paris. We will be able to see what it is like living there as a return trip for the pen-friend's visit to London (page 78). Paris is the capital city and largest city of France and Europe. Before we go there we need to know more about the country itself.

France is a big country twice the size of Britain. There are many contrasts in the land and the way people live. There are plains like those we saw in the Netherlands and mountains like those in Switzerland. There are fertile farmlands and big industrial cities. Map (1) shows six areas (regions) of France. Here are six descriptions, A to F. There are many clues which will help you match each description to an area on the map. Use a map of France in your atlas and the map on page 32 to help you.

A This region has the largest city in France. It is at the centre of a saucer-shaped lowland. Routes radiate to a ring of market towns and ferry ports. Farms are large, modern and mechanised. They supply the city with wheat, vegetables and dairy products. This is the most industrialised part of the country.

B This is a mountain area with snowfields, glaciers and forested slopes. It is a popular region for winter sports holidays. Sunny south-

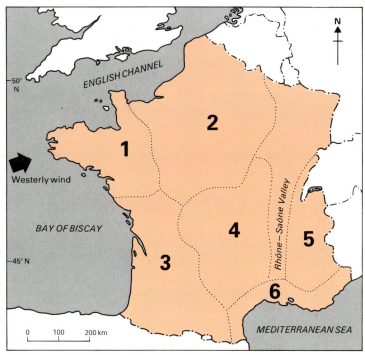

1 Regions of France

facing slopes are terraced for livestock and vineyards. Hydro-electric power is used for the aluminium and forest industries.

C This is a lowland with fertile soil. Winters are mild and summers are very warm so farmers can grow wheat and maize, peaches, melons and vines. Because the region is far from the capital, new ideas are slow to come to it. Farms often have small fields and mixed farming. One large inland town assembles aircraft. The main port handles half of all French wine exports.

D This region has a long rugged coastline and most towns are fishing ports, tourist resorts or naval bases in sheltered inlets. Winds from the Atlantic Ocean bring rain to the low granite hills. Being close to the sea, winters are mild but summers only warm. Walls protect the dairy herds, apple orchards and crops of early vegetables. There is a market for these products in Britain.

E Long hot dry summers, a sunny south-facing coast and a warm blue sea attract millions of tourists to this region every year. In winter it is warm and westerly winds bring rain but in summer farmers need irrigation water for their crops of wheat, maize, rice, vines, peaches, melons and vegetables. France's largest port is here. It is close to north Africa and the Suez canal. There are oil refineries and chemical industries.

2 A small area of south-east France

91

F   This is a volcanic plateau with ancient lava and granite rocks. Soils are poor. At over 1000 metres it is cool and damp and farming is for sheep, cattle and potatoes. There are forests and open moorlands. Young people are leaving to find work in other regions.

4 Coal miners

FOLLOW-UP WORK

1 For each region on the map say which one major feature makes the region different from the others.
2 With the extra help of map (3) do these.
   (a) Name the city in region A.
   (b) Name the port in region E.
   (c) Name the inland city in region C.
   (d) Name the port in region C.
   (e) Which region has most industry?
   (f) Name a region with little industry.
   (g) Which region uses solar energy?
   (h) Which region uses local supplies of HEP for aluminium refining and other industries?

   (i) Name two regions where photograph (4) could have been taken.
   (j) In which part of France is most steel made?
   (k) Paris has no local materials for industry but many industries are shown on map (3). Why do you think Paris is a good place for industry?

3 Industries of France

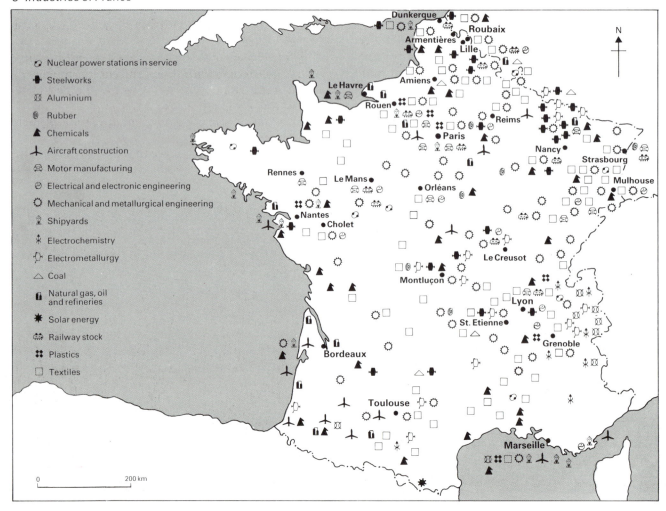

Paris

The best way to see Paris is from the air. View (5) is looking west across the centre of the city. You can see the river Seine. The first houses were built on the island in the river furthest from the camera. It is called Île de la Cité. There you can see the famous Notre-Dame cathedral. It is more than 800 years old and a church was there before that. Paris, like London, has a long history and was a Roman settlement.

On the right bank of the river there are historic buildings, shops, offices and the oldest houses in Paris. On the left bank is the university. The bookshops, printers, cafés and restaurants are for the students who come from all over France to study there. Now look back to page 78 and look at view (1) across the centre of London.

1 (a) In what way is the centre of London different from the centre of Paris?
  (b) Why is it helpful for both cities to be on the banks of large rivers?
  (c) Why do you think the first houses were built on an island in the river Seine?
  (d) Why do you think many of the houses in the centre of Paris need repairing?
  (e) Which city, Paris or London (see page 79), has the most parks near the centre of the city?
2 All the big companies in France have an office in Paris. More offices are needed. Look at these plans.
  Plan A. Knock down the old houses with their narrow streets and squares at the centre of the city (6). Build big office blocks and put car parks

5 A view across the centre of Paris

under each one. Make wide streets and more parks and gardens.
Plan B. Repair the old houses. Build a few office blocks (7), shops and entertainments near to the newer houses in the north, south, east and west parts of the city.
Plan C. Repair the old houses. Build one big area of office blocks with shops and entertainments in the west part of the city. This has the best road and rail links to the centre of the city.
(a) What are the good and bad things about each plan?
(b) Which plan do you like the best? Say why.

6 Old houses

7 New offices

You get good views all over Paris from the Eiffel Tower (8). It was built for the international exhibition in 1889. Its height, now it has a television mast on top, is 318 metres. There are viewing platforms at 58 m, 116 m and 276 m. If you go to the top you can see for 90 kilometres. You can see wide roads and railways spreading out to all parts of France like the spokes of a wheel (see the map on page 32). View (9) is from the first platform just 350 steps from the park below. You might take the lift instead.

9 *View from the Eiffel tower*

8 *Eiffel tower*

10 *Road network in Paris*

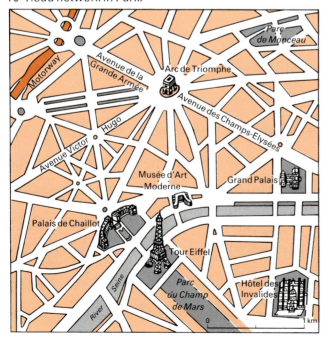

3 (a) When picture (9) was taken, was the camera pointing north-west or south-east?
   (b) What is the name of the large building in this picture?
   (c) Can you see office blocks in the distance? What does this mean for question 2?

4 Map (10) is the area west of photograph (5). On the right bank (north) of the river there are offices, shops and hotels. On the left bank there are government buildings. The wide roads were made in the second part of the nineteenth century. They took the place of whole neighbourhoods and a jumble of narrow streets. Even these wide roads are jammed with traffic in the rush hours. One million vehicles go in and out of the centre every day.
   (a) Why do you think traffic jams happen:
      (i) at the Arc de Triomphe;
      (ii) near the Eiffel Tower?
   (b) How is this pattern of roads different from Milton Keynes (page 90)?

Paris is the chief city of France. This is because it is on the banks of the river Seine and in the middle of rich farmland. It is also because people make it grow. Government and companies make decisions there, roads and railways lead there, companies want their factories, offices and shops there.

Young people go there to find jobs. They like the tree-lined avenues (11) and the shops and entertainments (12). They need houses, schools, hospitals and many other things. Young people soon have families of their own. And so the city grows and grows. Look at the figures in table (13) and map (14). They show how Paris has grown into a big city.

5 (a) What do you (would you) like and dislike about living in a big city?
(b) Draw a line graph to show how Paris has grown since 1800. Use the figures in table (13). The vertical scale can be 1 cm for 1 million people. The horizontal scale can be 1 cm for 20 years. What does your graph show?
(c) Copy map (14). Use colours to show the three areas of growth. Why do you think the city spreads out with 'fingers' in all directions?
(d) More people live in Paris than in London. London covers more land than Paris. Which city has the most crowded housing areas?

6 Your map shows how Paris spread like a pool of oil over the countryside. Table (13) shows that from 1980 to 2000 another two million people will live there. But now the growth will have a plan. You can make this plan by using table (16) and your own copy of map (15) on page 96.
Use your plan to answer these.
(a) Why is it better to have new cities than letting Paris spread outwards again?
(b) How many of the five new cities are *tied* to Paris?

11 *Along the Champs-Elysées to the Arc de Triomphe*

(c) Is this like the new towns around London (page 87)?
(d) Will traffic jams in Paris get worse? Say why.
(e) Draw onto your map a new road joining E3 to K6 and one joining E7, H10 and K10. How does this change the road pattern of Paris?
(f) What will happen to trees and farmland when these roads are built?
(g) Why is the new airport (J3) in a better place than the old airport (H8)?

13 *People living in Paris*

Year	Millions
1800	1.0
1850	2.2
1900	4.0
1920	5.8
1940	6.4
1960	7.6
1980	10.1
2000*	12.0
(*estimated)	

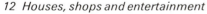

12 *Houses, shops and entertainment*

14 *Growth of Paris*

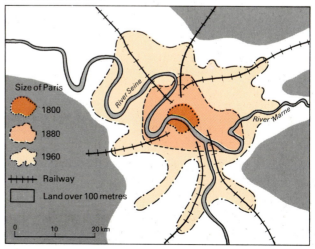

Size of Paris
1800
1880
1960
Railway
Land over 100 metres

River Seine
River Marne

0   10   20 km

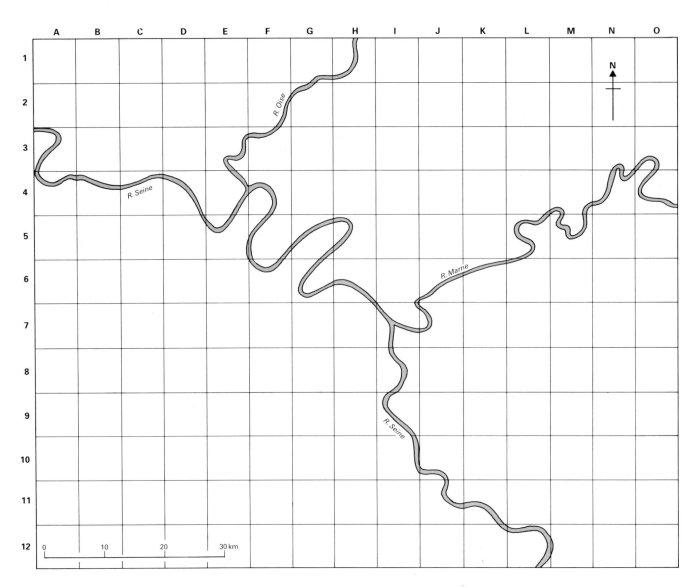

16 Information to plot on the map

Colour or symbol	Feature	Squares
Red	The centre of Paris	H6
Yellow	Housing areas	F5–7 G4–8 H4,5,7,9 I4–8 J4–7 K7
✈	Airports	J3 H8
Green	Woodland and forest	A2,3,5 B2,3,7,8,9 C5,8 D5,9,10,11 E5,6,8,10 F4,11 G2,3,11,12 H2,12 I1,2,9,12 J1,10,11 K1,2,12 L7,8,12 M7,8,11 N7,11,12 O12
Brown	New cities	K6/L6 D3/E3 D7/E7 H10/I10 K10,11

All other squares are farmland areas. Add a key to your map.